The Practice of Field Instruction in Social Work   Theory and Process

MARION BOGO   ELAINE VAYDA

The Practice of
Field Instruction in

Social Work

Theory and Process – with
An Annotated Bibliography

UNIVERSITY OF TORONTO PRESS
Toronto Buffalo London

© University of Toronto Press 1987
Toronto Buffalo London
Printed in Canada

ISBN 0-8020-6689-5

Canadian Cataloguing in Publication Data

Bogo, Marion
The Practice of field instruction in social work

Bibliography: p.
ISBN 0-8020-6689-5

1. Social work education – Canada. 2. Social work
education – Bibliography. 3. Social service –
Field work – Study and teaching – Canada. 4. Social
service – Field work – Study and teaching –
Bibliography. I. Vayda, Elaine J., 1927–
II. Title.

HV11.B64 1988   361.3′07′071   C87-094881-4

This book was first published in two volumes, *The Practice of Field Instruction in Social Work: Theory and Process* and *The Practice of Field Instruction in Social Work: An Annotated Bibliography*. Both were published in 1986 as part of a Field Instructor Training Project using funds provided by Health and Welfare Canada under Project No. 4563-4-19. They are here combined in one volume, somewhat revised and updated.

Contents

Field Instructor Training Project Network

University of British Columbia
Nancy Dickson

University of Calgary
Mary Valentich
Jack McDonald
Don Collins

Carleton University
Mary MacLean

Dalhousie University
David Williams
Gwen Fitzgerald

King's College
Ken Gordon
Elizabeth Pittaway

Lakehead University
Melanie Waite

Laurentian University
Richard Carrière
Michel André Beauvolsk

University of Manitoba
Ruth Rachlis

McGill University
Judy Magill

McMaster University
Sally Palmer
Ralph Brown

Memorial University
Marjory Campbell
Kathleen Cummins

University of Regina
Mike Simpson
Harlan Magneson

Ryerson Polytechnical Institute
George Bielmeier
Ellen Sue Mesbur

St. Thomas University
Sandra de Vink

University of Toronto
Marion Bogo

Wilfrid Laurier University
Herb Wiseman

University of Windsor
Margaret Meyer
Bernie Kroeker

York University
Elaine Vayda

Acknowledgements

This book was made possible by a generous grant from Health and Welfare Canada. This grant became a reality because of the advice, help, and encouragement of Robert Hart, Consultant, Health and Welfare Canada and Dr. Dennis Kimberley, former Executive Director of the Canadian Association of Schools of Social Work and co-author of Trends and Issues in the Field Preparation of Social Work Manpower, Part II, Policies and Recommendations. Our grant, Trends and Issues in the Field Preparation of Social Work Human Resources: Phase IV is sponsored by the Canadian Association of Schools of Social Work. We wish to thank Dr. Frank Hawkins, President of the Canadian Association of Schools of Social Work, for his active support and encouragement at crucial steps along the way.

Special thanks go to our network of participating schools, their deans and directors, and to all our project liaisons. Our own schools have provided continuing support and encouragement, in particular, Dr. Frank Turner, Director, Department of Social Work, York University and Dr. Ralph Garber, Dean, Faculty of Social Work, University of Toronto. In addition, we owe much to our students and field instructors who have shared our enthusiasm and have informed us through their comments, thoughts, and questions.

We are grateful to Imogen Taylor, who reviewed our manuscript and provided thoughtful editorial suggestions. We are pleased that Esther Blum accepted our invitation to write the chapter on ethnically sensitive field instruction. Finally, our thanks to Felicity Coulter, our F.I.T. Project secretary, whose patience, concern, judgment, competence, and hard work made our task infinitely lighter.

Introduction

The impetus for this book began with the publication, in 1980, of the findings of the study Trends and Issues in the Field Preparation of Social Work Manpower. This study canvassed field co-ordinators and field instructors connected with schools of social work across Canada to gather data about a variety of issues relevant to field education. One finding seemed to be persistent and consistent; namely, that field instructors felt a lack of preparation for the task they undertook when they agreed to take students.

The authors were able to convince Health and Welfare Canada to fund a project which would address this commonly expressed need for relevant preparation only after we could demonstrate that Canadian schools of social work shared an interest in this project and would appoint a special faculty liaison to the project. Thus, a network was established, comprised of representatives from eighteen schools across Canada. Issues, concerns, and specific information about the nature of the respective practica were solicited and disseminated. A consensus of this information was used by the authors to formulate the areas of field instruction that should form the basis of a book on field instruction written for field instructors.

It became apparent as we reviewed and discussed these issues, that field instruction is a branch of social work practice. We needed to develop an organizing principle of field instruction that would be applicable to all levels of practice, both direct and indirect, to traditional and non-traditional settings whether rural or urban, to BSW and MSW education. The model would have to be compatible with the unique educational philosophy and organization of the participating schools.

Our aim has always been to develop a generic model that is compatible with the unique aspects of specific schools of social work but would provide a structured approach for field instructors. We have deliberately omitted substantive social work theory and focused instead on the dynamics of teaching and learning in the field. It is the responsibility of the individual schools to communicate to field instructors their philosophical and theoretical approach. We have felt from the beginning that our model has international application.

The process of writing this book has been a challenge and a satisfying experience for both of us. Because we are both practicum co-ordinators for our respective schools, we had the opportunity to try out our ideas with our field instructors who shared with us excellent suggestions and their enthusiasm for the project.

We hope the field instructors who read and use this book will find the model and material helpful and responsive to their quest for adequate preparation to undertake the field education of social work students.

Marion Bogo, M.S.W., Adv.Dip.S.W.
Social Work Practice Professor
Field Practicum Co-ordinator
University of Toronto

Elaine Vayda, M.S.W., C.S.W.
Associate Professor
Field Practicum Co-ordinator
York University

1 Theory of Field Instruction

This book is directed to field instructors and faculty undertaking the task of helping field instructors define their role and learn their craft. Field instruction is a unique area of social work practice and is applied through an interactive process. We propose to describe and discuss the theoretical construct upon which field instruction is based and to develop the process of its application. Specific concerns of field instruction, such as the learning-teaching relationship, setting and monitoring assignments, and evaluation issues will be presented.

We begin with the premise that accreditation granted to an institution providing social work education guarantees that the curriculum is providing a practicum component. Field instruction, though derived from the school curriculum and from an older model of apprenticeship, is a unique approach to professional education which demands thoughtful preparation. Academic courses alone are not enough nor is an apprenticeship requirement per se sufficient to qualify for a social work degree. The field instructor must learn to travel a new road between the university system and the service provider.

Field instructors are those persons who are selected or who volunteer to guide students through the practicum requirement of the social work curriculum. They may be attached either to a community agency or service or may come from within the school itself. Effective field instructors should have current practice experience as well as a commitment to social work education. Neither a faculty-based educator with no direct involvement in practice nor a practitioner disinterested in the educational process is properly equipped to provide the guidance that is required.

Nomenclature can be confusing because various titles are used to describe persons engaged in field instruction, such as practice teacher, field instructor, field faculty, agency supervisor. In order to be consistent, the title of field instructor will be used throughout this book.

Regardless of title, it is the function of the field instructor that will be examined.

Educators in social work have always characterized the business of the practicum as the place where theory is integrated with practice. All too frequently this statement stands without further definition. Integration of theory and practice (ITP), without examination, may be a kind of magical incantation, through which educators, like alchemists, hope to transform a social work student into a professional social worker. Recognizing the limits of magic, even for social workers, we propose that the thrust of this book be to engage field instructors in the work of demystifying ITP and giving it operational meaning.

Adult learning theory builds on the premise that learning is stimulated by a problem which needs to be solved and is therefore firmly rooted in the practice experience. Kolb has suggested a four-stage cycle: (1) concrete experience is followed by (2) observation and reflection which leads to (3) the formation of abstract concepts and generalizations which leads to (4) hypotheses to be tested in future action which in turn leads to new experience.[1] Since experiential learning is directly related to immediate goals and needs, the learner is highly motivated to understand and solve the problem. The cyclical learning experience is both active and passive, concrete and abstract.

We have adapted this cycle to make it applicable specifically to social work education. The integration of theory and practice as process can be made visible through conceptualizing a looping phenomenon.

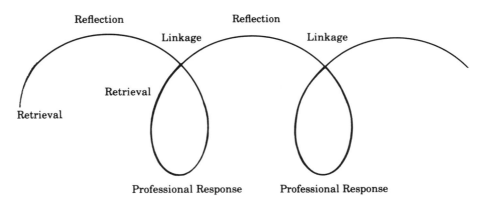

FIGURE 1: I.T.P. LOOP (INTEGRATION OF THEORY AND PRACTICE)

It is important to note that the loop can be applied to a wide spectrum of practice, both direct and indirect activities. It can be used to focus on a single interchange in a family therapy interview, for example, or the focus can be widened to examine a case management problem, or a neighbourhood analysis of significant actors in order to develop an effective strategy for community development. We believe the loop can be used to teach social work practice at any level of intervention, with a variety of populations, purpose, and setting. It can be microscopic or macroscopic depending on what facts are retrieved. The choice of a lens and the degree of magnification depends on the practice activity and the specific intent of the field instructor.

In this diagram, the process begins with the retrieval of the factual elements of a practice situation. The next step, reflection, focuses on the effectiveness of the retrieved interaction or intervention as well as the identification of personal values, attitudes and assumptions which modify the retrieved facts. These processes are then linked to professional knowledge that can explain or account for the findings of the preceeding steps. This leads directly to the selection of a professional response to the initiating action that began the loop.

The field instructor/practitioner will need to learn to use the ITP loop before it can be taught to the student. This requires that the instructor's own practice experience be subjected to the loop in order to become familiar with its applicability and flexibility.

RETRIEVAL

The entry point in the loop for the process of field instruction is the retrieval of the practice experience itself. It is the use of the observing ego, a "mind's eye" phenomenon wherein the social worker recalls a professional situation both as a participant as well as an observer. As a participant the role demanded interaction with the other participants, clients or relevant data. As observer, the professional role requires noting circumstances and setting, as well as a variety of modifying factors; interpersonal, cultural, economic, or political.[2]

REFLECTION

Reflection begins with consideration of the practice activity. This can be accomplished by reflecting on the effectiveness of the retrieved interaction or intervention and considering the impact on both the user system and the worker. In this way, reflection begins to build an ongoing evaluation of the work accomplished.

In addition, it is necessary to identify the values, biases, assumptions, and attitudes which attach to the observed facts in order to make them understandable within a personal context. Because values and assumptions modify observations, they must be acknowledged insofar as possible. Reflection, we believe, is what has more generally been called self-awareness. For example, cultural, class, and sex biases and assumptions must be identified so that their influence and power can be understood and controlled. Since the entry point in the loop is rooted firmly in the professional enterprise, reflection must always relate to the practice experience. While subjective, it is focused and purposeful and should not be generally invasive of a student's personality. Though the loop suggests that reflection precede linkage it would be equally effective to reverse the order and put linkage before reflection.

LINKAGE.

This step moves to a search for the professional knowledge base that makes it possible to choose a specific response to a situation from among a variety of competing responses. Schools of social work present to students a variety of theories and practice models which may include systems theory, developmental theory, role theory, social change theory, or a structural analysis of social systems. This list is not exhaustive. What is important is that a professional response is informed by knowledge.

The field instructor's task is not only to draw the student's attention to theoretical knowledge but also to help the student apply that knowledge in relation to a specific practice situation. What is stated in general conceptual terms must be made situation specific. We are not suggesting that the field instructor must teach theory which may already have been taught by the school. Students carry an overload of theoretical content from the classroom which they have difficulty transferring to practice. It is the concrete situation which makes it possible for the field instructor to help the student link knowledge in order to understand phenomena of practice.

Field instructors will identify their own knowledge base of practice. This base may or may not be the approach emphasized by the school of social work attended by the student. Differences in approach between the field instructor's practice and the emphasis taught in the contracting university can be acknowledged and in most cases reconciled. There may be several routes to a desired outcome. What is truly frightening for both student and field instructor is to be on the road without a map.

To prepare to use this part of the loop, field instructors need to look at their own practice. Retrieve a practice situation such as; work with a client system, staff supervision, community activity, or a policy and planning activity. Ask what informed the choice of approach, direction, or response. Professional behaviour is not random, but is an application of theory. It is not usually a pure application of a cognitive base but rather a distillation derived from compatible knowledge bases modified by the specific and immediate situation. This can also be described as theory in action. The task of field instructors is to think through their own practice in an analytic way in order to help students through a similar process.

PROFESSIONAL RESPONSE

This is the end of the ITP loop and also the beginning of the next phase. The field instructor and student try to select from the discussion in the linkage phase an appropriate professional response. It may be that several possible theoretical frames have been explored, each having its unique appropriate intervention. The student thus has an opportunity to make contrasts and to anticipate the possible effects of a specific intervention. A response or action is selected and its effect then becomes the focus of the same process. The use of ITP should facilitate the student's conceptual understanding of the situation which will result in an informed response to the practice situation as the contact continues. If field instructors use the loop after each encounter the student should feel a growing sense of control over the uncertain elements of practice.

Field instructors must be able to articulate this process so that what has become intuitive, a "gut" reaction response can be unwound. What is integrated must be rolled out and made visible step by step. Students struggle with the process of selecting an appropriate response to a practice situation from a bewildering array of options. The student can be led through the steps of retrieval, reflection, linkage, and response as the key to integrating knowledge with professional practice.

It is probably practice wisdom that leads social workers to use the ITP loop intuitively, but in many cases with omissions. The steps of retrieval and professional action, for example, are undoubtedly always operative, but we believe that either reflection or linkage may be omitted as practice competence becomes more routine. Since students need to think through their practice responses, they must be encouraged to go through the entire cycle. Both field instructor and student need to take the time to engage in reflection and linkage. Field instruction can teach an analytic process that begins with a practice act and moves through the loop. Through this process, the practicum can unite the apprenticeship model with the academic elements that lead to an integrated professional approach.

ORIENTATION TO THE LOOP MODEL OF FIELD INSTRUCTION

Begin at the beginning or start where the field instructor is remains sound social work advice. The beginning field instructor is a competent practitioner, so that, understanding the basis of one's own competency is essential to achieving the skill to guide the student through the necessary steps of analytical thinking.

The process of field instruction training includes the following:

1. Reflection on one's primary comfort as a competent practitioner along with an ability to tolerate residual discomfort.
2. The ability to retrieve elements of one's own practice behaviour and to subject these elements to critical self-analysis.
3. The ability to articulate this process, that is, to be able to say what was done and why it was done.
4. The ability to link practice behaviour to the value and knowledge base derived from practice experience and to articulate this linkage.

5. The ability to engage the student in the same process of retrieval, reflection, linkage, and response.
6. The ability to help the student build and reinforce a level of practice capability that will meet professional standards.

LEARNING TO USE THE LOOP

The worker recalls her own experience as a social work student when she could not tell her field instructor that she did not really understand what was meant when the instructor said, "*Look for and use what the client says and does not say.*"

Your approach to your student will contain traces of your own practicum experience, positive or negative, and will shape your concept of what you wish to convey to your student and what climate you feel you want to establish. Take the time to reflect upon your own experience and put it into words.

This process of preparation for the field instructor begins at the "point where the field instructor is"; that is, you begin by retrieval of elements of your own student experience. If your experience was a positive one in which you felt you learned and developed your professional practice through ITP, then you need to identify the elements of the relationship with your field instructor that promoted development and growth. Conversely, if your student field experience was unpleasant and not conducive to growth, retrieve the experience and reflect on those elements of the relationship with your field instructor that inhibited learning.

It is not essential that you share this process with your student, but it will increase your self knowledge and inform the structuring of your initial meeting with your student. Even though as a new field instructor you have a new set of anxieties, the process of retrieval will put you in touch with the anxieties and expectations the student brings to the initial meeting so that you can connect to them with empathy. You have retrieved your student experience and attached the recall of events and feelings to your new task as a field instructor. The retrieved material can then be focused and through the process of preparation linked to a body of field instruction knowledge via the ITP loop.

Practice is essential in order to become familiar with using the ITP loop.

The following hypothetical illustrations provide examples of how the loop can be used. Your own practice can be used to demonstrate the elements in the loop and to provide the experience you need before you introduce the loop to your students. Field instructors have found that this is not an easy task but is well worth the effort. If you can demonstrate the use of the loop to your student it becomes easier for the student to learn its application.

CASE EXAMPLES
Indirect Practice

The worker has been asked by the Ministry of Community and Social Services to submit a brief suggesting how scarce funds should be deployed in providing for the needs of the elderly.

Retrieval

1. Family caregivers, when interviewed, said if they had some relief from time to time they could manage to keep their relative at home.
2. In some instances modifications made to living accommodations have enabled some persons to remain in their homes.
3. Providing transportation to the elderly or to the caregiver for shopping and essential errands as well as for medical visits has facilitated home care.
4. There are wide disparities in the provision of and accessibility to support services across the province such as meals-on-wheels, telephone linkage, and emergency communication systems.

Reflection

1. The worker recalls that his grandmother lived with his parents and that he enjoyed her presence.
2. The worker holds the belief that institutions are impersonal and dehumanizing no matter how well run.
3. The worker has general positive feelings for the elderly based on personal experience.
4. The worker's feelings are consonant with the social work value of the worth of the individual.

Linkage

1. Economic and sociological theorists have argued that the elderly are devalued in our society because a premium is placed on productivity, mobility, independence, and economic power.
2. Studies of institutionalization suggest it may contribute to disorientation and dehabilitation wherein the victim is blamed for what are the consequences of the system.

Professional Response

The worker writes a brief for the Ministry which recommends funding of expanded home care aids for the elderly and the diversion of funds from additional nursing home beds.

Retrieval

1. The worker's report rejected options to improve nursing home facilities or to look for innovative alternatives such as co-operative group housing.
2. Responses to the report contain concern for those persons who will need

nursing home placement and those family situations in which an elderly relative could not receive adequate care.

The process of ITP looping has begun again.

Direct Practice

1. A child welfare student worker has received a complaint that children are being left unattended.

Retrieval

Unable to reach the mother by phone, the worker goes directly to the apartment. There is no response when the worker knocks on the door. A neighbour opens her door in response to the noise and peers at the worker. The worker can hear a child crying in the apartment but it takes five minutes before the door is finally opened abruptly by a woman who appears quite angry. The worker says, "I am Ms. B. from the Children's Aid Society. We have received a complaint that your children are being left unattended." The woman looks as if she might explode and shouts, "lies", to the worker. The worker asks if she can come in to talk about it but the woman slams the door in her face.

Reflection

The student was encouraged by the field instructor to reflect on the effect her unannounced arrival must have had on the client's reaction. She also speculated on whether the neighbour had heard what she said about the children being neglected and what effect this might have had in the matter. The student also realized that as she waited for the door to open, she became more and more uncomfortable. The field instructor suggested that she try to re-experience that uncomfortable feeling and speculate on its source. The student was able to talk about her distaste at having to confront the mother using the Children's Aid Society authority when she really wanted to establish a trusting relationship.

Linkage

The student is struggling with the role of authority vested in the Children's Aid Society worker and the apparent contradiction with social work relationship theory. The field instructor must identify the student's conflict in these terms and help the student to seek a way to reconcile the contradiction. This might be accomplished by looking for the positive aspects of authority as a means to engage that part of the parent's desire to protect and provide for her child. This process is derived from linkage with concepts such as reframing and establishing a working alliance.

Professional Response

The field instructor suggested that she and the student role play the next encounter with the mother which would provide the student an opportunity to try out alternate responses that incorporate the student's understanding of her conflict with authority and helping.

2. A student in a home for the aged is involved in a plan to bring together elementary school children and some residents of the home in a grandparent-tutorial program.

Retrieval

The student asked the school principal and the director of nursing to meet with him to discuss the plan. At the meeting, the student promises that he will organize and manage the program for four months when his practicum will be completed. The nursing supervisor smiles and says, "I don't think we do our people any service by getting them into something and then just dropping them." Though the student and the school principal continued to talk with enthusiasm about the project, the nursing director's resistance resulted in no further action and the meeting ended on an indecisive note.

Reflection

The field instructor recognized the student's confusion and disappointment that the program seemed to be at a dead end. On further reflection, the student said that he really had assumed that the nursing director would approve of the plan and he had set up the meeting without even meeting with her to explore her interest in the program. The student admitted that the nursing director's comment seemed to be a "put down" of him as just a student. He felt belittled by this woman and he had difficulty continuing with the meeting.

Linkage

The student ignored important aspects of organizational theory and program development. The field instructor reviewed with the student preliminary steps that should have occurred before the meeting he described took place. These steps might have included recognition of the need to discuss his proposal with the nursing director in order to tease out her concerns and gain her support. The field instructor also drew attention to the importance of program continuity and suggested that he had to give some thought to who would be responsible for the program after he left.

Professional Response

The student decided that he would seek out the nursing director and ask if she thought the program had merit and solicit her suggestions about how the program might be implemented and continued after he had left.

Notes

1 David A. Kolb, *Experiential Learning: Experience as the Source of Learning and Development* (Englewood Cliffs, New Jersey: Prentice Hall, 1984).
2 Retrieval can be used to consider the intake or initial facts of a practice situation in order to plan with the student for the actual contact.

The Triadic Nature of
Field Instruction

THE SCHOOL AND THE FIELD: DIFFERENT FRAMES OF REFERENCE

Field instructors carry their role within the context of two institutional settings, the school and the field. Each organization has different values, purposes, and processes. As well, each differs in defining social work practice, social problems, and appropriate interventions. These differences create a dynamic tension between schools of social work and social work service providers. Social work literature has specified the nature of this tension.[1] The following figure highlights differences between the two institutions.

Purpose

The purpose of the university-based school is to educate for practice, and contribute to knowledge building. Valued activities are research, scholarship, and teaching. The university's time perspective is primarily future-oriented. Schools' primary focus is analysis and critique of current forms of practice, and experimentation leading to new intervention approaches.

The purpose of the agency is to provide services to people in need. The valued activity is the delivery of effective and efficient service. The agency's time perspective is primarily present-oriented concerned with maintaining and enhancing current programs.

Expectations

Organizational expectations are reinforced through rewarding and sanctioning employee performance. In general, the university expects its members to employ critical analysis, to research and experiment,

	SCHOOL	FIELD
Purpose	Education Knowledge Building	Service
Valued Activities	Teaching Research Scholarship	Effective and efficient service delivery
Time perspective	Future-oriented	Present-oriented
Primary Focus	Analysis and critique of current practice Experimentation	Maintain and enhance current programs
Rewarded Behaviours	Critical analysis Developing, testing, reporting new ideas Independent activity	Competent job performance System maintenance Interdependent activity
Approach to Social Work	General Abstract	Specific Concrete

FIGURE 2: SCHOOL/FIELD: FRAMES OF REFERENCE
(Note: For purposes of illustration dominant trends are characterized as polarities. We recognize that social service settings often value and practice characteristics attributed here to the educational institution and vice versa)

and to function independently; therefore, individuality and autonomy are encouraged. Development, testing, and reporting of new ideas are rewarded.

The agency expects its members to perform their job function, as it is defined by the organization, in a competent manner. In general, the agency rewards members who work interdependently within the norms of the agency and contribute to system maintenance.

Approach to Social Work

The university addresses itself to social work in its general and broad sense. Its concerns are with the totality of the discipline of social work. As such its scope tends to be broad and abstract. Students learn knowledge and skills which are generic in nature and transferable to practice in a range of settings, with a range of client problems or social situations.

The agency addresses itself to a specific part of social work, embodied in a legislative mandate or a mission statement. The focus may be on a particular population, for example, children in need of protection, or an issue such as housing. Its scope tends to be particular and concrete. Students learn knowledge and skill reflective of the specific practice functions and client needs of that agency.

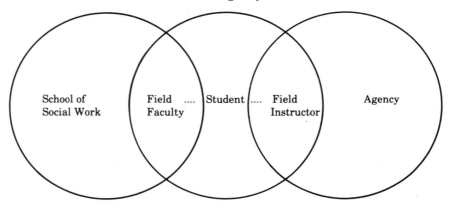

FIGURE 3: SCHOOL/AGENCY INTERFACE

Through participation as members of these respective systems, perceptions and behaviours are influenced by the organizational context. Increasingly, there is a tendency to adapt and conform to organizational expectations. To do otherwise risks isolation within or termination from the organization. For example, the worker who is often critical of agency practices may be labelled as a "trouble-maker." Similarly, the faculty member who teaches "what is" and does not critically examine practice will be labelled "unscholarly" by colleagues. Therefore, it is likely that faculty members and field instructors will have different perceptions and behaviours in respect to social work practice and education. This will manifest itself particularly as they work together in the field practicum.

Benefits, as well as tension, can develop from difference. Through dialogue one can come to a position of broadening and changing perceptions. Intervention models can be developed, tested, refined, and ultimately made more useful to people in need through collaboration between faculty and field. Social functioning can be enhanced through changes in policy and funding. Through use of the integration of theory and practice loop, practice behaviour can be retrieved, subjected to reflection and linkage, resulting in a modified professional response. In this way both university and agency contribute to the development of social work knowledge and practice.

Field instructors are part of the school and thus belong to two different organizations simultaneously. Students in the field practicum, faculty members carrying field responsibilities, and field instructors are participating in an activity which takes place in "two worlds" and is effected by both these contexts.

The differences in school and agency contexts may be experienced as a tension. It is useful to openly discuss the issues creating difficulty. The presence of unexpressed and unresolved negative feelings can lead either party to excessive criticism of each other, total avoidance, or unproductive alliances with students against the absent party.

THE CURRICULUM

Field instructors are often mystified by the school's curriculum as it relates to the practicum. Schools of social work develop their curriculum in accordance with the policies and guidelines established by their accrediting boards. The information in this section is based on Canadian Social Work education. Most Canadian schools of social work are members of the Canadian Association of Schools of Social Work. In 1970 the Association established an accrediting authority. The Accreditation Board has developed a limited number of general standards. Schools are expected to define educational objectives and to plan a curriculum to meet these objectives. A uniform curriculum model is not prescribed. Rather the development of clearly articulated curriculum objectives and design is expected. This policy enables the Canadian schools to develop programs responsive to their particular regional, professional, and university contexts.[2] As a result, considerable variation exists in social work programs offered in Canadian schools.

Social work programs are offered at the first university level resulting in the granting of a Bachelor of Social Work, and the second university level resulting in the granting of a Master of Social Work. The standards for each level are different.

Social work education at the first university level takes the form of professional studies within the context of general university education.[3] Graduates of such programs will be prepared for general practice which is defined as the application of basic social work knowledge to intervention in various sizes and types of social systems.[4] Graduates are expected to demonstrate at least beginning competence in arriving at professional judgments and actions, based on an integration of theory and practice within the context of professional values with respect to direct professional intervention with clients.[5]

The field practicum is expected to reflect the school's objectives, provide direct practice responsibilities for students, and ensure the educational purpose of the practicum is primary. Following these general standards each program will develop its own curriculum and structure for achieving the goals it sets out.

Social work education at the second university level should reflect graduate level university education and professional purpose.[6] The curriculum should allow for flexibility based on individual student's educational needs and interests.[7]

A graduate is expected to demonstrate the competence required of graduates of first-level programs. In addition, the competence of a graduate of a second university level program will include the ability to analyze, use, evaluate and develop theory in relation to complex practice situations within the context of a professional value base.[8] The graduate will be competent to enter direct and/or indirect practice.

Programs requiring a Bachelor of Social Work for admission shall include an opportunity for a practicum. Other programs shall require a practicum of all students.[9]

THE EDUCATIONAL EXPERIENCE OF THE FIELD INSTRUCTOR

Accreditation demands that social work programs engage in self-study which encourages responsiveness to changing practice and educational concerns. Therefore, curricula are constantly evolving. The curriculum that field instructors experienced as students may be different from the current focus of the school with which they are now associated. Using your experience as a starting point it may be helpful to compare the similarities and differences in respect to: program level, educational objectives including ideology and mission, curriculum design, core courses and elective courses, and how the practicum fits into the curriculum. A curriculum is a complex of objectives and design, often requiring extensive involvement to fully understand it. A general understanding is all that can be expected of a new field instructor, but this is sufficient to become familar with the student's academic experience.

ASSESSING ACADEMIC BACKUP

Field instructors frequently query whether the student "knows enough" to practice in their setting, whether the student has the appropriate knowledge base, and whether they are expected to teach theory. In contracting the practicum the field instructor should discuss with the faculty the practice and learning experiences in that setting. Together they can identify the knowledge base that will support field learning and determine whether that content is available in the school's current offering. For example, social work on a medical ward might include the opportunity to learn to work in an interdisciplinary model; to learn short-term, task-focused intervention with adults; to learn about community resources for disabled people. Knowledge about multi-disciplinary teams, the psycho-social impact of illness on individuals and families, crisis intervention, health policy and programs for the disabled would support field learning. Such a discussion might make it possible for the faculty representative to ensure that the student will take appropriate supporting courses.

It is helpful to engage students in a discussion specifying the experiences they bring that will facilitate learning in this setting. Students can reflect on volunteer and work activities, life experiences, and academic courses. In focusing this discussion on the learning opportunities that the practicum can provide, the student can identify useful and transferable knowledge and skills as well as existing gaps and determine whether these gaps can be addressed through academic courses. University courses tend to present material at a general level of conceptualization. For this material to be useful in the field a more specialized focus may be needed. For example, the student may have taken a course in social welfare policy but not have studied the specifics of health policy and programs affecting the disabled, the client group to be served in the field setting. A reading list can be developed to address gaps in the student's knowledge base. The faculty representative may be able to assist field instructors and students with this task.

Engaging the student in this process of assessment and planning can mark the beginning of the integration of theory and practice. Through retrieval of knowledge learned, reflection on that body of knowledge and skill in relation to its use in the current practicum, links between theory and practice, class and field are forged.

AN ECOLOGICAL PERSPECTIVE

Regardless of the primary thrust of the practicum setting, direct service, community or policy and planning, we feel that social work students should be required to consider their work from an ecological perspective that accounts for institutional pressures on people and includes activities designed to ameliorate those pressures.[10] We realize that the extent and scope of these activities will vary from setting to setting but some activity should never be omitted from a social work practicum. Such attention to the ecological framework is a hallmark of social work practice which differentiates it from other helping professions which rely on interpersonal relationships. Current social work texts stress a systems approach to assessment, intervention and evaluation of service, and students should bring to the practicum some understanding of the reciprocal nature of systems and their importance.[11]

Advocacy can be defined narrowly as activities undertaken to plead a client's cause or more broadly as creating bridges to facilitate understanding and responsive organizational change. Both definitions are important and are dependent on the specific situation. Students in the practicum need to be encouraged to see that in some situations their help to individuals, families, and groups will prove ineffective without considerable focus on organizational change.[12] Social work practice should be understood by students as a bridging profession that moves from a holistic perspective in assessment to focus attention on those parts of the system that may be contributing to the dysfunction of any specific part.

Brager and Holloway have developed a useful definition of organizational change that may be helpful to field instuctors in their search for ways to sharpen students' awareness of this dimension of practice.[13] They describe three types of organizational change; people-focused change refers to changes in the attitudes, knowledge, and skills of administrative and line staff; technological change refers to adjustments and responses in institutional programs and activities; and structural change is defined as changes which can occur in traditional relationships and roles which affect authority and responsibility as these are defined by the organization. Structural changes can be perceived as transfer or shifts in power and control.

Field instructors, starting again from the base of their own experience should examine their practice and that of other workers to identify examples of ecological activities directed toward organizational change either within their own agencies or within other institutions. These examples give specificity to students seeking to understand their role in this aspect of social work practice. Social work values which speak to enhancing human dignity and self-worth may then be transformed from vague, global, and passive words to concepts capable of serving as guides to planned activity in the service of client well-being.

Advocating for change can easily be omitted from the practicum as both student and field instructor focus on learning skills of interviewing and facilitating interpersonal intervention. Students are more anxious about these concrete skills and may designate the practicum as their skills laboratory. The danger lies in the separation of theory and practice residing in this narrow definition of the focus and purpose of the practicum. Unity of social work theory and practice should be a practicum goal.[14] The ITP loop can be helpful in ensuring a holistic and ecological approach because it insists that through linkage to professional knowledge, all knowledge be canvassed for guidance in selecting a professional response. In order to help students prepare for practice, field instructors should direct them to discover how decisions, both formal and informal, are made within the agency or institution. Instructors should discuss with students ways in which they can influence these decisions effectively and sensitively, how they can marshall the necessary facts to influence decisions through a planned

16

strategy, and how they can recognize and deal with resistance to change at any level. This is particularly important when the setting is not a primary social work agency but rather a secondary setting.

Advocacy has a role outside of the agency organizational structure, as well as within. Field instructors must direct students to become familiar with the community in which the agency is located. Prepared by this investigation, field instructor and student can discuss the social, economic, cultural or ethnic characteristics of the community, whether it has a cohesive or transient population or whether the housing is adequate or substandard. Students should be encouraged to explore the network of community resources available to meet the needs of the populations served by the agency. Such exploration may uncover needs for resources that the community does not provide. When a student identifies a need for which no resource exists, field instructors can guide students to think through strategies that may generate resource building to meet the need. Other interested workers or key figures in the community can be mobilized to join with the student in formulating a strategy. It is important that field instructors include this aspect of practice in the learning objectives that they and the student construct in order to ensure a holistic approach to social work practice. Such activity may lead to the formulation of services such as transportation for the elderly, or after-school activities for children of sole support parents.

Finally, students in some settings need to learn about socio-legal issues such as welfare appeals, Workers' Compensation Board appeals, immigration matters, or how patients are protected by mental health legislation. Students become interested in these matters when their application is immediate. Field instructors should encourage students to become knowledgeable in order to respond appropriately.

PRACTICUM OBJECTIVES

All schools have developed practicum manuals which state practicum objectives and procedures. These tend to be expressed in fairly general terms encompassing a variety of practice approaches with a range of client groups, target systems, or projects. Competency-based education gave impetus to a move to articulate objectives in clear, specific, and behavioural terms which could then be evaluated in assessing competence.[15] Again, we are faced with the difference between the university and the agency. The university, concerned with the totality of the discipline of social work, defines practice in general and abstract terms. Practicum learning objectives are often expressed in global terms. These objectives serve as a framework and guide in concretizing and specifying the learning objectives in any field setting. A particular student's objectives will be reflective of the agency practice. Agency practice is defined in relation to mandate, practice approach, client/target needs, and value positions. For example, all schools state in some form the expectation that the student learn assessment skills. The student engaged in community development in an outreach project on an Indian reservation will learn to assess even though the specific assessment skills may be different from those required by the student studying family therapy in a children's mental health centre. Both will have learned the general concept of assessment; specificity is based on the expertise, purpose, ideology, and model of the field setting.

Notes

1 Jerome Cohen, "Selected Constraints in the Relationships Between Social Work Education and Practice," *Journal of Education for Social Work* 13 (Winter 1977):3-7; Barbara Cowan and Edcil Wickham, "Field Teaching in University Context," *Canadian Journal of Social Work Education* 8(3 1982):81-86; Michael L. Frumkin, "Social Work Guidelines and the Professional Commitment Fallacy: A Practical Guide to Field School Relations," *Journal of Education for Social Work* 16 (Spring 1980):91-99; Barbara Thomlison and Susan Watt, "Trends and Issues in the Field Preparation of Social Work Manpower: A Summary Report," *Canadian Journal of Social Work Education* 6 (2 and 3 1980):137-158; Elmer J. Tropman, "Agency Constraints Affecting Links Between Practice and Education," *Journal of Education for Social Work* 13 (Winter 1977):8-14.

2 Canadian Association of Schools of Social Work. *Manual of Standards and Procedures for the Accreditation of Programs of Social Work Education.* Standards of Educational Policy, (Ottawa, 1983), p. 1.

3 Ibid., p. 2.

4 Ibid.

5 Ibid.

6 Ibid., p. 6.

7 Ibid., p. 7.

8 Ibid.

9 Ibid.

10 Carel B. Germain and Alex Gitterman, *The Life Model of Social Work Practice* (New York: Columbia University Press, 1980); Ruth Middleman and Gail Goldberg, *Social Service Delivery: A Structural Approach to Social Work Practice* (New York: Columbia University Press, 1975); Allen Pincus and Anne Minahan, *Social Work Practice: Model and Method* (Madison: University of Wisconsin, 1973).

11 Carolyn Singer and Lillian Wells, "The Impact of Student Units on Services and Structural Change in Homes for the Aged," *Canadian Journal of Social Work Education* 7 (3 1981): 11-28.

12 George Brager and Stephen Holloway, *Changing Human Service Organizations: Politics and Practice* (New York: The Free Press, 1978), pp. 18-19.

13 Ibid.

14 Elaine Vayda, "Educating for Radical Practice," *Canadian Journal of Social Work Education* 6 (Summer 1980): 102-106.

15 Morton L. Arkava and E. Clifford Brennan, eds., *Competency-Based Education for Social Work: Evaluation and Curriculum Issues* (New York: Council on Social Work Education, 1976).

3 Approaches to Field Instructions

"Students can only learn practice from very experienced competent practitioners."

"Students are adults and can learn if not interfered with by supervisors. They need to be allowed to be self-directed learners."

"Beginners need structure and need to be taught the basics before they try to work with clients."

"If you don't know who you are, your strengths and hang-ups, you can't help others."

These comments, made by field instructors, reflect a variety of assumptions about how students learn to become social workers and therefore what the focus should be in field instruction. While these quotes are idiosyncratic, they are representative of some of the approaches to field instruction that have been used in North American social work education. Analyses of approaches to field instruction have appeared in recent social work literature.[1] Though they are presented as ideal types, in actual practice, modifications and combinations are common.

APPRENTICESHIP MODEL

All authors note that, as in other professions, education for social work began with apprenticeship training. The apprenticeship approach in field instruction gives primary emphasis to learning through doing. Knowledge, skill, values, and attitudes are transmitted to the student through observing an experienced professional at work and observing, emulating, or modelling one's own behaviour on that of the field instructor. The instructor gives suggestions, directions, and coaching as the student learns to carry a practice role. This model emphasizes only two elements of the ITP loop, retrieval of the practice experience and formulation of a professional response. Traditionally process recording was used to access practice data.[2] Currently, instructors use audio and video tape,[3] observation mirrors,[4] observation or co-leadership of interviews,[5] committee meetings, programs, as well as written reports to examine practice.[6] Immediate feedback, including directions for alternate professional behaviours is given in settings that use direct supervision. Devices such as telephones and "bug-in-the-ear" may be used. Co-leadership or participant observation of practice activities also provides immediate alternatives.[7] Review of audio and video material[8] provides opportunity to discuss alternate responses and role play new behaviours for use in future practice encounters.[9] The instructor/ student conference, wherein practice wisdom and skill is passed on to the learner, remains central. The focus is on applying the instructor's practice knowledge to the student's practice assignments. These retrieval techniques are discussed in Chapter 7.

The apprenticeship approach appears to focus on behaviours and strategies, and to omit reflective and conceptual activities. The instructor is not specifically directed to help the student become aware of how their own values and assumptions can affect their perception of phenomena and their practice intervention. Nor is the instructor directed to help the student identify and use appropriate concepts from the professional knowledge base to understand phenomena and plan responses.

GROWTH – THERAPEUTIC APPROACH

Influenced by psychological therapies, and the human potential movement, an approach developed which gives considerable emphasis to self-development or personal growth as a necessary element in professional development. As well, this approach attends to the use of a professional knowledge base to guide professional behaviour. However, much attention is paid to the retrieval of observed facts and to considerable reflection on the student's feelings, thoughts, and attitudes elicited in those practice encounters.

This approach assumes that to facilitate growth and change for the client, the social work student must experience a personal growth process.[10] In addition, professional helpers must have a relatively high degree of self-awareness.[11] Kloh-Ann Amacher, reporting on an intensive study of students in field work, observed that:

When students learn about clients, they are learning about human beings...they are learning about themselves. They are learning how to understand behaviour, and understanding makes it manageable and less frightening. Increasing knowledge and skill, increased acceptance of human feelings and a growing sense of competence and mastery bring beginning security in the professional role and less need to distort perceptions of clients and self for the purposes of safety or to provide outlets for meeting the student's own needs ... Learning and achievement provide self-esteem and the safety necessary to grapple productively with the emotional and philosophical issues.[12]

Using this approach the field instructor gives considerable attention to the internalized and externalized manifestations of the student's past and present experience. Siporin notes the concern expressed in the literature that the educational process will become a therapeutic process.[13] Instructors are cautioned to deal with students' emotional difficulties only insofar as they interfere with learning. This creates an inherent dilemma. Students are encouraged to be reflective and disclose personal issues elicited by the social work process. When field instructors feel that the personal problems of students are interfering with service delivery and learning, they encourage students to seek help. At times it appears difficult for instructors, having explored and identified students' personal issues, to avoid attending to them in ongoing instruction. However, research on social work supervisees' and students' reactions to supervision found that a focus on personal issues was considered stressful and objectionable.[14]

Siporin comments that this orientation was cast aside during the '60s and '70s while greater attention was paid to political and social factors in assessing and intervening in problems of social functioning.[15] He identifies a need to re-introduce the concepts of self-awareness, self-discipline, and self-development within the current social and interpersonal contexts of practice, rather than in largely intrapsychic terms as in the past. For example, as students learn to practice with clients and communities from differing ethnic, class, or cultural groups, they need to become aware of the ethnocentric nature of their own values, and assumptions. Feminist analysis has directed attention to the need to raise consciousness regarding the inherent sexism in practice models.[16] As well, gerontologists have noted the prevalence of "ageism" in our society.

The reflection phase of the ITP loop calls for self-awareness and self-development in regard to psychological, socio-cultural, and political issues relevant to current ecological conceptualizations of social work.

ROLE SYSTEMS APPROACH

The role systems approach identified by Wijnberg and Schwartz[17] shares many similarities with the principles of andragogy as described by Malcolm Knowles.[18] The approach focuses on the transactional nature of the relationship between student and field instructor. The relationship is more egalitarian than in the approaches already presented. The basis for the relationship is less on psychological coercion and more on shared recognition of expertise and competence of both learner and teacher. The ideal learning climate is characterized by respect, openness, collaboration, and an expectation of active involvement in planning, implementing, and evaluating learning and progress in the field. The communication of positive and negative feedback is essential to provide the ongoing data necessary to modify the learning environment and practice behaviours. Role expectations of student and field instructor are arrived at through ongoing negotiations. The structure and process of educational and service components of field instruction are specified in considerable detail through formal or informal contracts.[19]

This approach focuses on negotiation of the structure, process, and content of field instruction. An instructor who uses the ITP loop with the role systems approach would begin by sharing the loop concept with the student, making explicit the teacher's belief and approach to field instruction. A pure application of the role systems approach would necessitate that the student agree to the use of the ITP loop. Student and instructor would then negotiate the various elements of field instruction so that the student's learning needs would be met.

ACADEMIC APPROACH

The academic approach emphasizes the student's cognitive development focusing primarily on knowing and understanding the professional knowledge base. The practice activity is viewed as providing examples of the theory learned in the academic setting.[20] Field learning in this approach often takes the form of a block practicum occurring after the student has learned a particular body of knowledge. It is assumed that the student will then be able to apply this knowledge to practice. The field instructor is expected to facilitate "an experience where the students test out their knowledge."[21] The field instructor is informed of course content, however the faculty representative carries the major educational responsibility. The focus is on using a professional knowledge base to direct professional responses or behaviour.

ARTICULATED APPROACH

Using the articulated approach the student must become "fully aware of what is involved in a practice act, know why that intervention is selected, and be prepared to determine how the necessary helping techniques should be performed. Beyond that, the art of the student's individual practice style takes over."[22] In presenting this approach, Sheafor and Jenkins argue for planned linkages between academic and field content wherein curriculum is carefully sequenced.[23] There must be full acceptance by faculty and field instructors of the content to be taught, as well as its relevance for practice in field agencies. Learning begins with introduction to a professional knowledge base, followed by practice. The knowledge base is then reviewed, and integrated using one's own style.

While there is considerable overlap with the ITP loop, this approach does not emphasize reflection as an activity. A structural arrangement between faculty and field is suggested which supposes that both agree on curriculum content, and plan and communicate frequently so that content introduced in both class and field is well timed and congruent. The authors note that the cost for both schools and agencies in using this approach would be greater than in other models.

During the 60s and 70s, federal government grants were available in Canada and in the United States which led to innovations in field teaching. Schools employed faculty-based field instructors to offer field education to units of students in traditional and non-traditional settings.[24] Field teaching centres were developed, staffed by personnel from faculty and field.[25] These units had a variety of objectives in relation to service and education. The goal was an articulated approach that linked academic content and practice.

It appears that these experiments which attempted to forge new structural relationships between academic and field learning are no longer prevalent in Canada. The Canadian study, *Trends and Issues in the Field Preparation of Social Work Manpower*, found that "92% of the field instructors were agency-based, compared with 5% who were faculty-based. Three percent of the field instructors did not consider themselves in either category and were in private practice, volunteered their time..."[26] Among the Canadian schools participating in the Field Instructor Training Project, it was found that this trend was still in evidence with the great majority of field instruction taking place with agency-based field instructors.

The articulated approach described in the literature is worthy of attention. However, many schools and field settings, faced with economic restraints, do not have the resources to design and implement such programs. We suggest that there are other ways to help students achieve the goal of knowledge-directed practice. A field instructor who is able to articulate the knowledge base from which their own practice derives and can help students do the same can achieve this goal as well.

COMPETENCY-BASED APPROACH

Competency-based education defines learning objectives in specific, observable, behavioural terms; designs learning activities and teaching approaches that ensure mastery of those skills; and develops evaluation measures to use in assessing student learning in relation to the original objectives.[27] Considerable attention has been given to the use of this approach in classroom[28] and laboratory[29]. Larsen and Hepworth report on their use of a competency-based approach in teaching task-centered practice.[30] In a comparative study they found that students taught in this method performed at a higher overall level of competency and had more confidence in their skills than those taught in a "traditional" approach.

The method consists of an initial selection of a discrete number of skills to be mastered and defines them in specific behavioural terms. The method of practicum instruction should focus on teaching these skills in instructional sessions through "analyzing (and teaching students to analyze) moment-by-moment transactions recorded in individual, group, couple, and family sessions. Particular emphasis was accorded to the efficiency, appropriateness, and facilitativeness of specific student responses."[31] This approach was contrasted with "traditional" instruction which was "less systematic, less task-focused, more global, and more focused on case dynamics than on student performance and skills level."[32]

This approach focuses on concretizing a particular professional knowledge base in the form of measurable behaviours. It appears little attention is paid to reflection based on the student's own experience.

Figure 4 summarizes this review of field instruction approaches in respect to the emphasis each approach places on what we have defined as the main components of field learning in the ITP loop.

ELEMENTS OF THE ITP LOOP

Field Instruction Approaches	Retrieval	Reflection	Linkage to Knowledge Base	Professional Response
Apprenticeship	X			X
Growth		X		
Academic			X	
Articulated	X		X	X
Competency-Based	X			X
Role Systems	Wherever instructor and student choose to focus			

FIGURE 4: A COMPARISON OF EMPHASES IN FIELD INSTRUCTION APPROACHES WITH THE INTEGRATION OF THEORY AND PRACTICE LOOP

Notes

1 Aase George, "A History of Social Work Field Instruction: Apprenticeship to Instruction," in *Quality Field Instruction in Social Work*, eds. Bradford W. Sheafor and Lowell E. Jenkins (New York: Longman, 1982), pp.37-59; Lowell E. Jenkins and Bradford W. Sheafor, "An Overview of Social Work Field Instruction," in *Quality Field Instruction in Social Work*, eds. Bradford W. Sheafor and Lowell E. Jenkins (New York: Longman, 1982), pp. 3-20; Marion H. Wijnberg and Mary C. Schwartz, "Models of Student Supervision: The Apprentice, Growth, and Role Systems Models," *Journal of Education for Social Work* 13 (Fall 1977):107-113.

2 Esther Urdang, "On Defense of Process Recording," *Smith College Studies in Social Work* 50 (November 1979): 1-15.

3 Rae Meltzer, "School and Agency Co-operation in Using Videotape in Social Work Education," *Journal of Education for Social Work* 13 (Winter 1977): 90-95; Bonnie C. Rhim, "The Use of Videotape in Social Work Agencies," *Social Casework* 57 (December 1976): 644-650; Barbara Star, "The Effects of Videotape Self-Image Confrontation on Helping Perceptions," *Journal of Education for Social Work* 13 (Spring 1977): 114-119; Barbara Star, "Exploring the Boundaries of Videotape Self-Confrontation," *Journal of Education for Social Work* 15 (Winter 1979): 87-94.

4 Regina Kohn, "Differential Use of the Observed Interview in Student Training," *Social Work Education Reporter* 1 (September-October 1971): 45-46; Vernon C. Rickert and John C. Turner, "Through the Looking Glass: Supervision in Family Therapy," *Social Casework* 59 (March 1978): 131-137.

5 Kohn, "Differential Use of the Observed Interview in Student Training," pp. 45-46; Marjorie Litwin Schlenoff and Sandra Hricko Busa, "Student and Field Instructor as Co-Therapists," *Journal of Education for Social Work* 17 (Winter 1981): 29-35; Edith Schur, "The Use of the Co-Worker Approach as a Teaching Model in Graduate Student Field Education," *Journal of Education for Social Work* 15 (Winter 1979):72-79.

6 Lynn Videka-Sherman and William J. Reid, "The Structured Clinical Record: A Clinical Education Tool," *The Clinical Supervisor* 3 (Spring 1985): 45-62.

7 Schlenoff and Busa, "Student and Field Instructor as Group Co-Therapists," pp. 29-35.

8 Rhim, "The Use of Videotape in Social Work Agencies," pp. 644-650.

9 Paul Abels, "Education Media and Their Selection," in *Teaching and Learning in Social Work Education*, ed. Margaret Pohek (Council on Social Work Education, 1970); Donald Collins and Marion Bogo, "Competency-Based Field Instruction: Bridging the Gap Between Laboratory and Field Learning," *The Clinical Supervisor*, forthcoming; Jo ann Larsen, "Competency-based and Task-Centered Practicum Instruction," *Journal of Education for Social Work* 16 (Winter 1980): 87-94.

10 Virginia P. Robinson, Ed., *Jessie Taft: Therapist and Social Work Educator* (Philadephia: University of Pennsylvania Press, 1962), pp. 246; 329.

11 Gordon Hamilton, "Self-Awareness in Professional Education," *Social Casework* 35 (November 1954): 371.

12 Kloh-Ann Amacher, "Explorations into the Dynamics of Learning in Field Work," *Smith College Studies in Social Work* 46 (June 1976): 199.

13 Max Siporin, "Teaching Marriage and Family Therapy," *Social Casework* 62 (January 1981): 20-29.

14 Alfred Kadushin, "Supervisor-Supervisee: A Survey," *Social Work* 19 (1974): 289-297; Aaron Rosenblatt and John E. Mayer, "Objectionable Supervisory Styles: Students' Views," *Social Work* 20 (1975): 67-73.

15 Siporin, "Marrriage and Family Therapy," pp. 23-26.

16 Cleo S. Berkun, "Women and the Field Experience: Toward a Model of Non-Sexist Field Based Learning Conditions," *Journal of Education for Social Work* 20 (Fall 1984): 5-12.

17 Wijnberg and Schwartz, "Models of Student Supervision," p. 3.

18 Malcolm Knowles, "Innovations in Teaching Styles and Approaches Based on Adult Learning," *Journal of Education for Social Work* 8 (Spring 1972): 32-39.

19 For examples of elements to be negotiated see: Marion Bogo, "Field Instruction: Negotiating Content and Process," *The Clinical Supervisor* 1 (Fall 1983): 11-12; Wijnberg and Schwartz, "Models of Student Supervision": 111-112.

20 Jenkins and Sheafor, "Overview of Social Work Field Instruction," p. 15.

21 Ibid., p. 16.

22 Ibid., p. 17.

23 Ibid., p. 18.

24 Carolyn B. Singer and Lillian M. Wells, "The Impact of Student Units on Services and Structural Change in Homes for the Aged," *Canadian Journal of Social Work Education* 7 (1981): 11-28.

25 Eustulio Benavides III, Mary Martin Lynch and Joan Swanson Velasquez, "Toward a Culturally Relevant Field Work Model: The Community Learning Centre Project," *Journal of Education for Social Work* 16 (Spring 1980):55-62; Helen Cassidy, "Structuring Field Learning Experiences" in *Quality Field Instruction in Social Work*, eds. Bradford W. Sheafor and Lowell E. Jenkins,pp. 198-214; Dorothy E. Moore, "Help Line: An Integrated Field-Research Learning Experience," in *The Dynamics of Field Instruction*, (New York: Council on Social Work Education, 1975).

26 Susan Watt and Barbara Thomlison, "Trends and Issues in the Field Preparation of Social Work Manpower: A Summary Report," *Canadian Journal of Social Work Education* 6 (2 and 3 1980): 5.

27 Morton L. Arkava and E. Clifford Brennan, eds., *Competency-Based Education for Social Work: Evaluation and Curriculum Issues* (New York: Council on Social Work Education, 1976), p. 17.

28 Ibid.; Betty L. Baer and Ronald C. Federico, eds., *Educating the Baccalaure-*

ate Social Worker: Report of the Undergraduate Social Work Curriculum Development Project (Cambridge, Mass.: Ballinger, 1978).

29 Stephen F. Canfield et al., "A Laboratory Training Model for the Development of Effective Interpersonal Communications in Social Work," *Journal of Education for Social Work* 11 (Winter 1975): 45-56; Collins and Bogo, "Competency-based Field Instruction"; Jo Ann Larsen and Dean Hepworth, "Enhancing the Effectiveness of Practicum Instruction: An Empirical Study," *Journal of Education for Social Work* 18 (Spring 1980): 50-58; Judith Magill and Annette Werk, "Classroom Training as Preparation for the Social Work Practicum: An Evaluation of a Skills Laboratory Training Program," *The Clinical Supervisor* 3 (Fall 1985): 69-76; William Rowe, "Laboratory Training in the Baccalaureat Curriculum," *Canadian Journal of Social Work Education* 7 (3 1981): 93-104.

30 Larsen, "Competency-Based and Task-Centered Practicum Instruction," pp. 87-94; Larsen and Hepworth, "Enhancing the Effectiveness of Practicum Instruction," pp. 50-58.

31 Larsen and Hepworth, "Enhancing the Effectiveness of Practicum Instruction," p. 52.

32 Ibid., p. 53.

4 Contributions from Educational Theory

Theories of human growth and development have spawned a plethora of related theories and practices about how children and adults learn and how teachers teach. Substantial research exists demonstrating the effectiveness of specific approaches. This chapter summarizes selected concepts which appear to be transferable to and useful in social work field education.

ADULT EDUCATION

The work of Malcolm Knowles who applied the principles of andragogy to social work education, is of particular relevance to field instructors.[1] He defined andragogy as "the art and science of helping adults learn."[2] He argues that adults learn better experientially, can be involved in analyzing their experience, and tend to have a problem-centered orientation to learning.

The purpose and structure of the practicum provides the environment for adult learning. It is problem-oriented, presenting the student with a situation requiring action which must be subjected to evaluation and re-evaluation. While self-direction, initiative, responsibility for one's own learning are expectations, at no point does Knowles suggest abdication of the intense involvement of the teacher with the student. Thus, the learning/teaching team of student and field instructor engage actively together.

Knowles suggests that the characteristics which promote an optimal learning climate are "informality, mutual respect, physical comfort, collaboration rather than competition, openness, authenticity, trust, non-defensiveness, and curiosity."[3] He says that one must have a clear notion of the competencies required for performing the social work role which must be applied diagnostically to determine the student's present level of development of these competencies. The competencies are categorized according to "knowledge, understanding, skill, attitudes, values, and interests."[4] The steps which follow diagnosis include; formulating objectives, planning a sequential design of learning activities, conducting the learning experience through mutuality and sharing the experience, and, finally, evaluating the learning. About evaluation, he states that "the only valid assessment of learning, especially in professional education, is performance in the carrying out of the professional role under either real or simulated conditions."[5] Evaluation should lead to re-diagnosis of the required competencies. In effect, all of the principles of andragogy describe an optimal practicum outlining the tasks and approach of field instruction.

LEARNING STYLE

Field education is frequently the most individualized form of teaching that a social work student will experience. The student and field instructor are likely to meet in regular, face-to-face, one-on-one sessions. The intensity of the dyad will highlight idiosyncracies of style and individual preferences of both participants regarding learning and teaching. The individual characteristics are important features influencing the success or failure of the endeavour.

Educational theory and research have demonstrated that individuals have different patterns or styles. "The term 'learning styles' refers to a student's consistent way of responding and using stimuli in the context of learning."[6] It describes the predominant and preferred approach which characterizes an individual's attitude and behaviour in a learning context. Hunt states that learning style describes a student in terms of those educational conditions under which he is most likely to learn.[7] It describes how a student learns, not what he has learned. Hunt believes the concept of learning style is a useful way to characterize interpersonal communication in education.

Many characteristics make up a person's learning style such as a preference for structure or non-structure, method or intuition, the concrete or the abstract, the active or the reflective, individual or group learning, visual, auditory, or tactile modes, self-directed or teacher-directed approaches. An extensive body of research and literature exists which describes these characteristics. We have chosen to focus on a selected number of learning style characteristics relevant for field instruction.

A knowledge of learning styles assists student and instructor to determine how a student learns best and how this pattern may differ from that of the field instructor. It also is useful in helping student and instructor design facilitative educational environments. As well, it directs attention to learning characteristics not favoured by the student that may need to be developed to make optimal use of available learning opportunities.

Berengarten's Learning Patterns

Sidney Berengarten writing in 1957, identified patterns in social work students' approaches to learning in field practice.[8] The "doer" learns primarily from repetitive experience in carrying out assignments. These students learn from active and direct teaching and need the instructor's help to conceptualize practice. The "intellectual-empathic" learner needs to conceptualize before acting. These students are self-directed learners, reflective, imaginative, and self-aware. The "experiential-empathic" learner initially reacts in a personalized manner to the practice situation and evidences stress and anxiety. These learners respond to the instructor's efforts to engage them in reflection and conceptualization. Since Berengarten's work investigators have carried out extensive research on cognitive style.

Conceptual Level

David Hunt has written extensively about conceptual level which describes students in terms of their requirements for structure in an educational environment.[9] "Highly structured environments are teacher-centered, include pre-organized material, and involve very specific instructions and expectations. Approaches which are low in structure are more likely to be determined by the student, involve general instructions, and include material which is not pre-organized."[10] Hunt observes that the degree of structure a person needs is related to a particular situation and their stage of development. Students new to social work education faced with learning the complexities of practice in multi-faceted situations may be expected to require considerable structure in the early phases of their training. As students develop more knowledge and skill they may need less structure in the educational environment.

Field Dependent/Field Independent

Witkin and his associates developed the concept of field dependent/field independent.[11] The concept refers to a global versus an analytic way of perceiving. It entails the ability to perceive items without being influenced by the background. Persons who are heavily influenced by the surrounding field are called field dependent; those who are relatively uninfluenced by the surrounding field are called field independent. Research has demonstrated that field dependent people learn material more easily if it has social content; favour people-oriented vocations, such as social work and education; are strongly influenced by authority figures and peer groups; and are more affected by criticism with regard to their learning. In comparison, field independent people are less sensitive to social cues; favour analytically oriented vocations, such as mathematics, engineering, science; and are not particularly affected by criticism.

There are a number of important implications from these findings. Field dependent students are likely to rely on their environment for cues as they learn new information. They are more dependent on feedback about their learning and progress than are field independent students. They give more credence to the authority and expertise of the instructor than the field independent student who is less concerned with field instructor availability and feedback. Field dependent students are more sensitive to criticism and therefore relationship issues such as the relative presence of empathy and acceptance from the instructor take on added importance.

Christine Marshall recently studied social work students' perceptions of variables which facilitated their learning in the practicum.[12] Variables identified included feedback that is ongoing, specific and constructive, and a relaxed atmosphere of mutual openness, acceptance, respect and trust. The facilitative instructor is available, empathetic, and sensitive to the students' differing needs for dependence and independence.[13] These findings suggest that the characteristics associated with field dependent learners were also identified as important by the sample of social work students studied.

It may be that we attach a pejorative meaning to the word dependent, seeing it as a negative quality that should not be promoted because it connotes lack of initiative and self-reliance. Field dependency, however, implies a level of greater comfort with a responsive social environment that provides supportive criticism. Social work, among other person-related professions, may attract more field dependent people precisely because the tasks to be performed demand responsiveness to social cues with a secondary emphasis on analytic skills. This suggests to field instructors that learning is facilitated by ongoing, constructive and specific feedback and may be impeded by an aloof "ask me when you need help" response adopted to encourage independence.

Matching

Interest in learning styles has led to considerable debate regarding the benefits of matching students to learning environments. Research on primary and secondary school children shows that learning style matching has a positive impact on student achievement, interest, and/or motivation.[14] Yet, studies where personality characteristics were matched reveals that in some cases a disparity between teacher and student personality is the vehicle for maximizing student growth.[15] For example, Hunt found that teachers who operate at a somewhat more abstract level on an abstract-concrete continuum can increase students' levels of conceptual complexity.[16] Studies where matching occurred to maximize congruence or similarity on personality characteristics reveal inconsistent findings.[17] Similarly, research to determine which teaching methods are most effective for a particular individual has not produced significant findings. Positive results have been found where students examined their own needs and goals, evaluated their learning style preferences, and teaching styles were provided based on these stated preferences.[18]

Hyman and Rosoff caution against a static view of learning and teaching styles.[19] They point out that teaching and learning is a dynamic interrelationship between teacher, student, and subject matter, in a particular environment, at a particular point in time. The student-teacher relationship changes as it develops and adapts to these multiple elements.

The educational theorist, Herbert Thelen, stated that "the learner does not learn unless he does not know how to respond."[20] Educators have attempted to address the issue of the optimal level of discomfort or comfort in producing an effective learning environment. There is a need to provide supportive and comfortable environments so that learners will risk themselves. However, as Rogers points out, our natural tendency as learners is to confine ourselves to those domains where we feel safe.[21] To promote growth, teachers have to help students reach into new and fearful domains, acknowledge discomfort, and set learning tasks to overcome the barriers of fear. Hunt, in stressing the relationship of the environment to development, observes that if the environment is perfectly matched to the developmental level of the learners they are likely to be arrested at that level.[22] Optimal mismatch challenges a student's tendency to maintain familiar patterns, encourages movement to a new level, but does not overwhelm and immobilize the student.

Research in teacher training revealed that teachers were able to learn new theories and skills in training sessions, but experienced considerable discomfort in using new approaches in their practice.[23] The great majority never tried the unfamiliar strategy unless support personnel were available. Subjects able to manage the feelings of discomfort attendant to new learning tended to use the new skills more frequently.

Joyce concludes that too much harmony between the learner and environment creates comfort that does not challenge growth.[24] He suggests that rather than match approaches to minimize discomfort, teachers need to generate a 'dynamic disequilibrium' that will expose students to new teaching approaches that may be uncomfortable to them. Joyce's comments can be applied to social work students who are learning new skills and expected to demonstrate those behaviours to field instructors through co-working, tapes or one-way mirrors. Students often report anxiety and discomfort with these new learning approaches. Matching theory suggests that instructors help students acknowledge and manage this 'threat to their comfort' while holding them to the use of new learning approaches.

Application

How can contributions from learning style theory be used by the field instructor and student? Friedman and Alley present principles for use by classroom teachers which we can adapt for our purposes.[25]

Instructors can identify their own preferred learning styles through reflecting on past learning experiences, and identifying what was effective and what was not. Simple paper and pencil tests can also assess characteristics of learning style.[26] Discussion with an agency supervisor or peers may provide useful insights. Often, learning style and teaching style are closely connected. That is, our teaching approaches are based on what we think we need in order to learn. Instructors can reflect on whether there is congruence in this respect.

Student learning style preferences can be identified through discussion, reflecting on past learning, observation of what is effective and what is not in producing learning, and simple paper and pencil tests. Instructors can examine the extent to which the learning environment provides educational opportunities that are responsive to the student's preferred learning style. This includes, the methods and approaches used in field instruction, as well as opportunities in the setting for activities such as observation, participation, and role play.

Students can be encouraged to diversify their learning style preferences and to participate in educational activities that require development of less preferred learning approaches. For example, the student who learns best from a thorough reading and understanding of the literature before action can be asked to take action in role play first and then identify learnings from the experience.

Notes

1 Malcolm Knowles, "Innovations in Teaching Styles and Approaches Based Upon Adult Learning," *Journal of Education for Social Work 8* (Spring 1972): 32-39.

2 Ibid., p. 32.

3 Ibid., pp. 36-37.

4 Ibid., p. 38.

5 Ibid., p. 39.

6 Charles S. Claxton and Yvonne Ralston, *Learning Styles: Their Impact on Teaching and Administration* (Washington, D.C.: American Association for Higher Education, 1978), p. 7.

7 David Hunt, "Learning Style and Student Needs: An Introduction to Conceptual Level," in *Student Learning Styles: Diagnosing and Prescribing Programs* (Reston, Virginia: N.A.S.S.P., 1978), Chapter 3.

8 Sidney Berengarten, "Identifying Learning Patterns of Individual Students: An Exploratory Study," *Social Service Review 31* (December 1957): 407-417.

9 Hunt, "Learning Style and Student Needs."

10 Ibid., p. 8.

11 Herman A. Witkin, "Cognitive Style in Academic Performance and in Teacher-Student Relations," in *Individuality in Learning*, Samuel Messick and Associates (San Francisco: Jossey-Bass, 1976).

12 Christine Marshall, "Social Work Students Perception of Their Practicum Experience: A Study of Learning by Doing" (Ph.D. dissertation, University of Toronto, 1982).

13 Ibid., pp. 224-225.

14 Linda H. Smith and Joseph S. Renzulli, "Learning Style Preferences: A Practical Approach for Classroom Teachers," *Theory into Practice* (Winter 1984), p. 49.

15 Ibid., p. 45.

16 David Hunt, *Matching Models in Education: The Co-ordination of Teaching Methods with Student Characteristics* (Toronto: Ontario Institute for Studies in Education, 1970).

17 Smith and Renzulli, "Learning Style Preferences," p. 46.

18 Ibid.

19 Ronald Hyman and Barbara Rosoff, "Matching Learning and Teaching Styles: The Jug and What's in It," *Theory into Practice* (Winter 1984), pp. 39-40.

20 Herbert Thelen, *Education and the Human Quest* (New York: Harper and Row, 1960).

21 Carl Rogers, *On Becoming a Person* (Boston: Houghton Mifflin, 1951).

22 Hunt, "Matching Models in Education."

23 Bruce Joyce, "Dynamic Disequilibrium: The Intelligence of Growth," *Theory into Practice* (Winter 1984), p. 27.

24 Ibid., p. 29.

25 Peggy Friedman and Robert Alley, "Learning/Teaching Styles: Applying the Principles," *Theory into Practice* (Winter 1984).

26 David Kolb, *Learning Style Inventory* (Boston, Mass.: McBer and Co., 1975).

5   Anticipating the Practicum

THE NATURE OF UNCERTAINTY

The ends actually achieved in field instruction are determined by the means employed.[1]

Both field instructors and students contemplate the beginning of the practicum with anticipation and reservation. For field instructors, students bring many advantages and serve multiple needs. Students provide a break in the routine of practice, they can provide intellectual stimulation and a fresh view of practice as well as reinforcing a sense of practice competence. On the negative side, however, field instructors worry about how much time they will have to commit to the student and whether they will be equal to the task. Doubts are raised about being able to teach the student enough, about getting along together, and about the best kind of relationship to establish. Both students and field instructors feel the basic anxiety of any new interpersonal experience, namely, whether each will understand the other.

Social work is a profession in which the practitioner as a person is the instrument of intervention. This fact creates heightened anxiety for both field instructor and student. Our knowledge base is diffuse and demands an integration of concepts from several different disciplines. Though other professions, such as medicine, nursing, or law, demand interpersonal skills, they have, in addition, precise and visible technical skills which must be learned and applied, but which have no counterpart in social work practice. Kadushin has pointed out that students become anxious because they begin to perceive that change may be required that can affect not only their ideas but their behaviour and quite possibly their personality.[2] The combination of the diffuseness of the knowledge base, added to what is perceived as demands on personality itself, can quickly undermine the student's sense of adequacy and self-esteem.

The Student's Perspective

The beginning social work student has up to this point been socialized to relate to others with politeness, to desire to be seen by others as helpful and likeable, to respect the personal and private space of others, in short, to be a "nice" person. This is the internalized image of self which most students bring to the practicum. As the practicum develops, the student is aware that this is not a "good enough" self to bring to work with clients. Probing into another's personal space, hearing and responding to fears, pain, anger, sadness, and ambivalences are essential to developing into a competent social worker and these demands create a dissonance which threatens comfortable behaviour patterns and personality integrity. It is important that field instructors empathize with students' confusion and anxiety from the beginning of the practicum in regard to the newness of the social worker role contrasted with their image of themselves as a helping and kind person. This supportive attitude will form the cornerstone of the learning/teaching relationship. Charlotte Towle speaks of relationship as a means to learning which should develop the identity of the learner rather than obliterate it.[3] The process of self-awareness sets in motion continuing behavioural change in the direction of increasing receptivity and perception. Gordon Hamilton, writing in 1954, observed that self-awareness in professional education is a by-product which is a form of attendant learning rather than primary learning.[4] She felt that it occurs by increasing the student's capacity for self-acceptance. The field instructor should approach the problem of stimulating self-awareness on the level of conscious motivation. In other words, promoting self-awareness is related to the needs of client situations and is not to be presented as a therapeutic intervention with the student's personality. Self-awareness is essential for the student, but it is a by-product of the analysis of the experience of intervention.

In addition, many students with no prior work experience approach the practicum as another classroom course since this is their only analogous reference. They expect to be given a structure similar to a course outline or syllabus. They need to be introduced to the expectation that they must play a very active role in the learning/teaching relationship. Students may have received orientation from their schools that prepares them for the active participation expected in the practicum. Field instructors should take responsibility for discussing this expectation with students as soon as possible to avoid the frustration of misunderstanding.

The Field Instructor's Perspective

Self-awareness is also important for field instructors. Gizynski points out three areas where field instructors need to develop self-awareness.[5]

The first is the appropriateness of dependency needs. Some field instructors react with panic to students who look to them as omnipotent with all the answers. A common reaction is to try to pull away, to retreat from such devouring need. The student, however, sensing this withdrawal may become even more anxious and the cycle continues. With self-awareness, the field instructor may offer realistic reassurance, support, a sense that the student is not alone, which may help to allay the anxiety. Some field instructors may bask in this dependency, encourage it and feel let down when and if it diminishes.

The second area cited by Gizynski is that of differences in style. For example, a very active, confronting field instructor can be quite critical of a more passive, withholding student. Conversely, a low-keyed instructor can be put off by a more aggressive student. The trick is to be aware of your own style as a manifestation of your own personality and not as representing the most effective approach to a practice situation.

Thirdly, Gizynski refers to awareness of values. There are differences in attitudes toward, for example, sexual behaviour, drug use, and child care practices and styles. Such attitudes should never go unexamined and unacknowledged. Agreement is not essential but it is important that values be identified so that behaviour based on these values can be seen as choices made with as full an understanding as possible of the positive and negative consequences of each choice.

STRUCTURE: THE FIT OF LEARNING AND TEACHING STYLES

In Chapter 4, we discussed learning and teaching styles and suggested that the field instructor and student identify their own preferred styles. These preferences, used with caution, can provide a useful guide to the establishment of a workable fit between field instructor and student. Some students approach the practicum with the hope that the field instructor will dispel all their confusion about social work practice and will teach them how to be a social worker. Such students, though adult, may want to assume a very passive role in relation to an active teacher who will tell them directly how the job is to be done. Conversely, some students will approach the practicum feeling apprehensive about losing a sense of adult autonomy and will want a field instructor who will encourage independence.

Teaching Styles

In general, field instructors may be divided into three distinct groups. The first group of field instructors may feel very comfortable with a directive stance telling the student what to do step-by-step and checking frequently on the student's execution of these directions. The second group of field instructors may suggest mutual goal setting through ongoing negotiation with the student leading to a consensus. The field instructor plays an active role but demands equal involvement and responsibility from the student. The third group of field instructors may expect the student to be able to articulate goals and initiate and plan the learning experience using the field instructor as a consultant when needed.

Matching and Mismatching

Both matches and mismatches of directive or non-directive field instructors with dependent or independent students will occur. It is important, therefore, that these approaches be introduced and discussed early in the practicum so that a clear understanding of expectations and preferences can be uncovered. Even a mismatched pair, once identified, can attempt to reach a workable resolution. Self-awareness can begin at this point. For example, a field instructor who wants more feedback than an independent student may provide, can remind the student that, "I feel more comfortable when I am in touch with all of our cases." Or in response to the student who wants to check out every move with the field instructor, "I know you can make that decision on your own once you are clear about options."

Normally, as the practicum progresses and the student is learning at a satisfactory pace, the structure will relax so that the student is functioning with more autonomy than at the beginning of the practicum. This increasing autonomy can become an articulated goal which is set at the beginning of the practicum. The student might measure one aspect of growing competence through the increase in autonomous practice over a period of time.

CLIMATE

Climate refers to the nature of the relationship between field instructor and student. Rogers believes that significant learning is dependent upon the presence of certain attitudinal qualities in this relationship.[6] First is the quality of realness or genuineness, being aware of your thoughts and feelings, able to live with them, and communicate them to the student if appropriate. Next is an attitude of trust, respect, and acceptance of the other as a separate person, having worth. Finally, there is empathic understanding, the ability to accurately and sensitively listen to and understand the student within their own context and experience, and communicate that understanding to the student. Knowles strives for a relationship characterized by informality, mutual respect, physical comfort, collaboration rather than competition, openness, authenticity, trust, nondefensiveness, and curiosity.[7]

Research on field instruction shows that students perceive a relaxed atmosphere of mutual openness, acceptance, respect and trust as helpful to learning;[8] warm and understanding supervisors were found to be helpful in reducing student concerns compared to cold, aloof, and even hostile supervisors whom students reported did not allay anxiety but on occasion exacerbated students' fears and worries.[9]

Social work educators have also discussed the need for a climate conducive to learning characterized by the qualities presented thus far. Manis argues for openness and freedom, an atmosphere that lacks fear, makes explicit issues that were implicit, lacks compulsion and dependency, and encourages participation in decision-making.[10] Siporin states that the qualities of understanding, acceptance, and support are necessary to produce a collaborative and complementary relationship.[11] These qualities are basic to the practice of social work. When they are present in the field instructor-student relationship, the student experiences congruence between what is taught and how it is taught.

Barriers to Facilitative Relationships

In actual practice we often experience these qualities as ideals toward which we strive and often fall short. Three issues in particular mitigate against achieving ideal conditions in the field instructor-student relationship. They are perceptions about the power of the field instructor and the vulnerability of the student; the student's and the instructor's need for approval; and the transfer into the current relationship of assumptions and feelings developed in other, similar, relationships.

Students are realistically dependent upon the field instructor's professional expertise, knowledge of and access to the setting, and power of evaluation. A variety of interpretations of the extent of this power have been noted. Some students perceive the instructor as having so much power and themselves so little that they feel vulnerable at the hands of the instructor. They report feeling concerned about the instructor's potential to harm them. They expend considerable energy on trying to "figure out" what will please the instructor and to behave in accordance with those perceptions. This position mitigates against an atmosphere that is open, free, and facilitative of learning. Many writers note that field instructors have initial difficulty with the authority inherent in their role.[12] They feel uncomfortable with the evaluative power granted to them. Some may avoid using their authority, act as if it is non-existent, and create a 'buddy' relationship with the student. Others may respond in an authoritarian, constrictive, and rigid manner. There is a power discrepancy between student and field instructor which needs to be acknowledged, clarified in operational terms, and re-clarified through the ongoing process as misperceptions, confusions, and misunderstandings arise.

Both student and field instructor share the human need for approval, a sense that one is accepted and liked. The task of field instruction is to learn practice. The role of the field instructor is, among other behaviours, to give both positive and negative feedback, to help the student critically evaluate their own practice behaviours. Some students may experience negative input as a withdrawal of approval, feeling a loss of self-esteem and sense of adequacy. The instructor will be perplexed as the student has requested direct and clear feedback and yet reacts in an upset manner when it is given. Similarly the field instructor wants to help the student and be approved of as a 'good' instructor. This may lead to a tendency to give support and encouragement, and avoid challenge and confrontation, overlooking areas that need to be developed. Both instructor and student may feel comfortable with this pattern which maintains the status quo but does not promote development.

The concepts of transference and countertransference may be useful in furthering our understanding of relationship dynamics. These terms originating in psychoanalysis, have been used in clinical social work and have been more or less accepted or rejected through social work's long and stormy history with psychological theories. For the purpose of this discussion we would like to borrow the concept and use it, not in a therapeutic context, but in its broader, more generalized meaning as a description of a phenomena of human behaviour. In this respect transference and countertransference refer to those thoughts, perceptions, feelings, attitudes, and behaviours which are part of the personalities of both students and instructors, derived from their own significant relationship experiences, and activated by the intensity of the present relationship. They may appear to be non-rational, or inappropriate for or not related to the reality of the current situation. If only looked at from a surface perspective they are not easily understood. Transference and countertransference can be both positive and negative in nature. The transfer of positive feelings regarding growing, learning, nurturing and helping individuals develop can facilitate and catalyze a student-field instructor relationship. Negative transference and countertransference reactions can also appear connected to previous experiences with authority which were characterized by fear, vulnerability, and the power to harm. Unresolved feelings, transferred from such experiences and not related directly to the present situation, can lead the student or the instructor to behave in a manner not appropriate to a climate of participation and mutuality.

As in any social system, the student and the field instructor together, through their ongoing transactions, create a dynamic relationship. Each affects and is affected by the behaviour of the other. Through a process of reciprocal responses, patterns develop which create and maintain a unique climate for each dyad.

Case Example

Prior to entering a social work degree program, Jim G. had worked for four years in the welfare department as a caseworker. In his final year he had contracted to do his practicum in a family-oriented agency. He had contracted with Sally F., his field instructor, for 'direct supervision' where the instructor would participate in the interview sessions with him and intervene in his work with the client system as she thought appropriate. They would discuss the case process and their interventions after the session. As they were entering the interview room for the third family session, Jim turned to Sally and said, "Would you please just observe today. Let me carry the session myself." Sally was very surprised and said to Jim in an irritated tone, "Well, in that case, you don't need me in the room. Just tape the interview and I'll see you at our next meeting." She noticed he looked uncomfortable, as if he wanted to respond. She turned her back and went to her office.

Sally sat in her office and thought about what had just happened. She identified that she was feeling angry and rejected by Jim's sudden breaking of their agreement that she would participate in the interviews. She asked herself what was it that she was so angry about. She had tried to be a 'good' field instructor, sensitive to the student's need for control as an experienced worker. She had developed an approach to field instruction that emphasized mutuality and participation. In his rejection of this approach she felt 'unappreciated' and de-valued. She acknowledged that feeling appreciated is important to her in interpersonal relationships. She began to speculate about Jim's possible reasons for not wanting her in that session. She drew on her knowledge that all behaviour has meaning and is the product of reciprocal interactions. She concluded that if their relationship is to continue in a productive fashion, they must both be involved in resolving this impasse. She decided to explore with Jim at their next meeting his reasons for abruptly changing the terms of their agreement. In this way she did not continue to 'react' with anger to the incident, rather she chose a professional response.

When Sally introduced the topic at the next session she began by sharing her reactions to his request. Jim was then able to describe how her critique of his handling of a previous interview had left him feeling unsure that he had any ability as a social worker. Sally was astonished to learn that what she thought was clear, direct feedback could have such a devastating effect. She decided to explore his past experience with positive and negative feedback. Jim told her that as an untrained worker he had been very sensitive to feedback from supervisors fearing that he would lose his job if he was not 'good enough'. In fact he had received almost no negative feedback from his busy and preoccupied supervisor in the welfare department. It appeared that he had transferred into the current relationship thoughts, assumptions, and fears about job performance that were inappropriate to the educational task. These perceptions had effected the way he received feedback about his competence. His fear about dealing with authority manifested itself in attempts to control his instructor's input and perceived potential to harm him.

Based on this information Sally suggested they review their contract in order to clarify the expectations each has of the other. Through this discussion they articulated the differences in performance expectations between a learning situation and an employment situation. They also examined the difference between a field instruction and job supervision relationship. They clarified that Jim needs to feel validated in what he does know in addition to receiving feedback about what he does not know. As Jim left the office Sally felt pleased that she had responded to her concern that 'something was going on' that had provoked such strong reactions on both their parts.

THE INITIAL MEETING

Some schools insist on an initial meeting between the student and the field instructor as an essential part of the negotiation process prior to the decision to embark on the practicum. This is an important meeting and should be anticipated in a thoughtful way by both field instructor and student. Either the student or the school should provide the field instructor with a resume which contains basic information that can then be expanded in the interview. As with all preliminary information, the field instructor can make some tentative speculations drawn from the student's age, education, work and volunteer experience, and level of the requested practicum. The field instructor should have decided whether it is important that the student already have some skills in place or whether basic skill development can be one of the goals of the practicum. Some field instructors enjoy the challenge of working with an inexperienced student where the work of the agency makes it possible to accommodate these learning needs.

The content of the interview will generally be focussed on why the student wishes to learn in that particular setting, what relevant work, or volunteer experience and academic courses the student brings to the practicum, and the nature of the student's long-range social work goals. The field instructor should be prepared to answer questions about the nature of the agency and the type of experiences that can be provided to the student. It should be remembered that first-level students may find it more difficult to respond to questions about what they want to learn and may make very general statements that seem vague and uninformed. Students are accustomed to academic courses in which a curriculum is presented to them and therefore cannot make the adjustment quickly to the practice focus. The ITP loop is helpful here, because students may not have learned the relationship between theory and practice and how to connect the two. Some students, however, seem put off by questions about theory and seem to fumble as if they have had no conceptual exposure. Again, it may be that the integration aspect has never been emphasized, so theory and practice remain relatively unrelated. Second-level students are likely to be far more specific about learning objectives.

It is always a good idea to check on whether the expectations students have about what can be accomplished match with the reality of what can be offered as student experiences. In addition, field instructors should inform students of their expectations. For example, direct service field instructors might prepare students for the use of audio-visual facilities and live supervision via one-way mirrors. Indirect service field instructors might advise students to be prepared for week-end work, travel and public presentation. Because of the importance of learning and teaching styles, field instructors might ask students how they would describe themselves as learners. For example, do they prefer considerable direction or, in general, prefer to find their own way? Students might also be asked what facilitates their learning, that is, do they like to learn from reading, from discussion, or directly from experience. These are, of course, general tendencies and are not mutually exclusive. Field instructors will have concluded that this is a full agenda for an initial interview. Because most interviews take on a life of their own, these suggestions can only serve as guides.

For the field instructor, the first impression made by the student is a decisive factor in determining whether or not to proceed with the practicum. First impressions condense a multitude of factors and can produce strong feelings that are either positive or negative. The ITP loop may be useful in examining these reactions. For example, suppose you retrieve your observation of poor eye contact, a markedly passive manner, and clothes which seem to you inappropriate to the occasion. Reflection leads you to recognize that the student's ethnic background may be one in which deference to authority is expressed by passivity and avoidance of a direct gaze, characteristics which make you uncomfortable. Theory linkage tells you that the capacity for interpersonal relationships is critical for all levels of practice. You consider whether the student might learn relationship skills, and you make a decision based on weighing all considerations. We all respond positively or negatively to specific characteristics as irrational and unrelated to the task as weight and height, patterns of laughter and speech, awkwardness, age, and manifestations of sexuality. If you feel strong antipathy toward a student, you will probably decide not to accept that student. In those schools in which a preliminary meeting is not expected or is not possible, these guidelines should shape your first meeting with the student.

If your decision is to accept the student and it is a mutual decision to proceed with the practicum, you and the student have already begun the relationship which is so critical to the success of the practicum. However, if your decision is negative, you may feel uneasy about conveying this to the student. Some field instructors feel comfortable with telling the student why they feel it would not be a good experience for the student in that particular setting. Others may be able to ask the field co-ordinator to inform the student about why they cannot do that practicum. The student may also have reservations and may feel relieved about the decision. Whether a negative decision is discussed directly by the field instructor or indirectly through the field co-ordinator, insofar as possible, it should be a learning experience for the student. It is always important to inform the field co-ordinator about the nature and outcome of the interview.

Notes

1 Francis Manis, *Openness in Social Work Field Instruction: Stance and Form Guidelines* (California: Kimberly Press, 1979), p. 11

2 Alfred Kadushin, "Games People Play in Supervision," *Social Work* 13 (July 1968): 23-32.

3 Charlotte Towle, *The Learner in Education for the Professions* (Chicago: University of Chicago Press, 1954), Preface xv.

4 Gordon Hamilton, "Self-Awareness in Professional Education," *Social Casework* 35 (September 1954): 371-379.

5 Martha Gizynski, "Self-Awareness of the Supervisor in Supervision," *Clinical Social Work Journal* 6 (Fall 1978): 202-210.

6 Carl R. Rogers, *Freedom To Learn* (Columbus, Ohio: Charles E. Merrill, 1969), p. 106-112.

7 Malcolm Knowles, "Innovations in Teaching Styles and Approaches Based Upon Adult Learning," *Journal of Education for Social Work* 8 (Spring 1972): 32-39.

8 Christine Marshall, "Social Work Students' Perceptions of Their Practicum Experience: A Study of Learning by Doing" (Ph.D. dissertation, University of Toronto, 1982), p. 140.

9 Aaron Rosenblatt and John E. Mayer, "Objectionable Supervisory Styles: Students' Views," *Social Work* 20 (May 1975): 186.

10 Manis, *Openness in Social Work Field Instruction*, p. 16.

11 Max Siporin, "The Process of Field Instruction," in *Quality Field Instruction in Social Work*, eds. Bradford W. Sheafor and Lowell E. Jenkins (New York: Longman, 1982), pp. 175-197.

12 Lillian Hawthorne, "Games Supervisors Play," *Social Work* 20 (May 1975): 179-183; Kadushin, "Games People Play in Supervision," pp. 23-32; Susan Matorin, "Dimensions of Student Supervision: A Point of View," *Social Casework* 60 (March 1979): 150-156; Rosenblatt and Mayer, "Objectionable Supervisory Styles: Students' Views," p. 186; Lawrence Shulman, *Skills of Supervision and Staff Management* (Itasca, Illinois: F.E. Peacock, 1982).

6   The Beginning Phase

ORIENTATION

Once the decision to accept a student for the practicum has been made, field instructors can prepare the way for the arrival of the student. Sometimes the decision to accept a student has been made with the participation of the staff or team members. Consequently others will know about the student and may even be prepared to take part in the learning plan for the student. In other settings, the decision may be made only by the field instructor and so some advance planning is necessary. Other workers should be informed as well as support staff. It is helpful to have space already selected and prepared, and necessary supplies gathered. If it is a large agency, there may be bureaucratic forms and rituals that must be set in motion. There are distinct advantages for both the student and the field instructor in this preparatory activity. The field instructor has signalled to the agency that the student is to be a part of the agency's total function and is not only a singular appendage and responsibility of the field instructor. For the student, such preparation produces a sense of having been anticipated, expected and welcomed by the agency. A welcoming note, flowers, a name plate, are all tangible evidence of belonging.

In a secondary setting, preparation by the field instructor assumes even more importance. Hospitals, schools, or correctional facilities are complex and special care has to be taken to inform key persons, such as nurses, principals, department heads and support staff about the student's arrival, learning needs and timetable. Such planning paves the way for the student to follow up and establish important connections.

Some settings have established policies regarding the identification of students per se by requiring students to wear identification plates which signify their status as student social workers. This usually occurs

46

in hospitals where it is customary for personnel to wear some identification. Other settings require students to be introduced to clients as student social workers. Obviously, if your agency has established a policy, this must be presented to the student who then is expected to conform to that regulation. If no specific policy exists, field instructors should think through the implications for clients of specific designation as a student social worker and make a decision that gives the student clear direction. Clients should know who will be involved in discussing their situation and having access to information concerning them.

The day the practicum begins has arrived at last. How should this first day and week be structured? The field instructor must establish the right balance between information overload and the perception on the part of the student of neglect and lack of direction. A balance is also needed between the needs of the inexperienced, dependent student and the student who can take some initiative in getting needed information from the field instructor and others. If possible, field instructors should plan to spend time during that first day with the student, preferably when the student arrives, outlining the activities and plans for that day and week. Beginnings, as we know, are significant, and there is nothing so undermining of the heightened sense that accompanies a beginning as hours of neglect, confusing directions, or offhand, unthoughtful suggestions for activity.

Orientation can be both formal and informal, and is both substantive and interpersonal. Formal orientation should contain information on relevant legislation mandating and regulating the practice in that agency. It should provide instruction on required procedures both in regard to clients and to personnel policies. It should focus on the process of decision making in the agency which requires some understanding of the organizational plan from board, to executive director, to supervisory personnel and staff. Some field instructors encourage or require students to make opportunities to interview key personnel to get some concept of the range of services provided by the agency. Some settings, such as child welfare or large mental health facilities have established orienting sessions for new staff and students to familiarize them with terminology, and procedures specific to these settings. Students in such settings need to be encouraged by field instructors to take the time to learn unfamiliar words and procedures which they could not be expected to understand at the outset of a practicum. If field instructors do not themselves provide this structured and substantive orientation, they should remember to discuss the process with the student to clarify and augment what can be a confusing mass of information not easily digested until seen in context.

The informal and interpersonal aspects of orientation are a continuation of the preliminary preparation of staff already begun by the field instructor. Introductions to other key personnel and staff should be made. Students might be encouraged to note key names. Some attention should be paid to physical orientation if the agency is large, especially key locations such as washrooms and lunch rooms. Lunch routines are particularly important so that students feel specifically included and made to feel welcome. It makes a difference if there are several students or only one. Expected attendance at staff meetings or team meetings should be clarified with the student, along with some discussion of how they are expected to participate. The thrust of the orientation is to encourage students to perceive themselves as members of the social work staff with as many of the privileges and responsibilities as the circumstances of a specific setting will permit.

LEARNING CONTRACTS OR AGREEMENTS

What is a Learning Contract or Agreement

Social work literature reflects the acceptance of a concept of contract development both in work with clients and in field instruction. We feel that agreement might be a better term because contract has a legal connotation for many people. Field instructors should feel comfortable in selecting either word.

A learning contract is a document developed by the student and field instructor which specifies what and how a student will learn within a given period of time. The contract describes the structure of the practicum in respect to: end goals or objectives, actions or learning experiences to be used to arrive at objectives, and measurements or indicators of how the participants will know when the goals have been achieved. Though based on the field objectives of the school, the contract individualizes a student's learning program in a particular agency. The contract will explicate the roles and norms for participation of the partners in field instruction.

Formulating a learning contract involves a process, the end product of which is the written contract. Contracting engages both student and instructor in observation and retrieval of practice behaviour, reflection about that behaviour, linkage to a professional knowledge base and to the outcome objectives expected by the school. Through this process the field instructor and student can assess the student's base level of competence and plan a learning experience that will facilitate growth. Formulating the contract serves to shift the role of the field instructor away from that of "all-knowing expert" toward that of a partner in planning student learning. Significant learning takes place as a product of this process. The contract, once written, can serve as a stimulus to further assessment and planning as it is used to measure accomplishment at points in the practicum.

Why Use Learning Contracts or Agreements

The past decade has witnessed a growing attempt on the part of the profession and educational programs to define competent social work practice.[1] Schools of social work have defined competency expectations of students' learning in the practicum. These expectations tend to be defined in more or less specific behavioural terms. Students need ongoing assistance in assessing their level of skill in relation to these competencies. Contracting serves the purpose of assessment and indication of the student's performance level in relation to the outcome objectives. The contract formalizes in explicit terms what the student needs to work towards. It does so not only at the general level expressed in the school's practicum manual, but at the specific level that reflects the professional behaviours and activities in the particular field setting. This provides students with the opportunity to link the abstract to the concrete. The specificity inherent in such a contract enables students to participate more actively in the evaluation of their own learning. A number of writers in social work field instruction highlight the importance of the contract.[2]

Contracting is supported by research findings regarding adult learning. Allen Tough found that when adults go about learning something naturally, as contrasted with being taught something, they are highly self-directing.[3] Evidence seems to indicate that what adults learn on their own initiative they learn more deeply and permanently than what they learn by being taught. In traditional education the learning activities tend to be structured by the teacher. The student is expected to comply with the directives regarding how a body of knowledge is to be approached and how evaluation of learning is to be achieved. This encourages dependency, passivity, and acceptance which may be in conflict with the adults' need to be active and involved in shaping their own experiences. Since contracts are developed mutually students feel more involved in the learning activity.

Knowles notes that learning from a field experience contains elements of personal development as well as specific skills and attitudes demanded for entry into the social work profession.[4] Learning contracts provide a means for negotiating a reconciliation between these external needs and expectations and the learner's internal needs and interests.

Students entering social work education with limited familiarity of the field will need to learn how to participate actively in designing the contract. They will need to learn how to define what is to be learned. With some students, field instructors will have to be more directive in developing the contract until the student is more knowledgeable about what needs to be learned.

Knowles notes that the modern educational system is characterized by teachers telling students what and how they are to learn. When faced with a different educational process, that of mutual involvement in designing a learning program, students become anxious, confused, and worried. Therefore, field instructors need to pay attention not only to the content of contract construction, but also to the student's comfort with this process.

Educational theorists, in general, and social workers, in particular, have been concerned with an apparent contradiction between humanist values and stating measurable behavioural objectives for students. Humanists are concerned with the complexity of behaviour, its variety, and the nature of the "unexpected" in human dynamics. Learning, to be a human endeavour, must accommodate the uniqueness of experience and should not be made to fit into an instructional unit stated in behavioural terms which may become mechanistic and focused on demonstration of discrete performance skills. Pratt, a learning theorist, argues that the controversy has been too polarized and he believes that both training and education are important functions, certainly of social work education. He suggests that training be defined as "instruction which develops some permanent capability or state" and education as "the provision of significant or intrinsic experiences."[5]

How to Develop a Learning Contract or Agreement

It may be helpful to consider two very different kinds of contracts, one which may be easily drawn up at the beginning of the practicum if it is deemed desirable, and a second learning contract, which involves time and process, and cannot be drawn up until the practicum is underway.

The first type of contract can be termed a working contract. Some schools provide a field instruction manual which contains guidelines pertaining to the expectations and responsibilities of both field instructor and student. If such a manual is not available or if the setting is new or non-traditional, a working contract can provide specific agreement about time commitments, physical requirements, and a clear statement of roles and responsibilities. Even if a manual is provided, it may still be important to draw up a specific working agreement that reflects the actual circumstances of the practicum setting so that expectations can be mutually expressed.

The second type of learning contract is used to develop a specific plan for the practicum identifying the objectives, the means available to meet those objectives, and the methods to be used in determining when those objectives have been met. It provides a clear focus for the practicum, which is explicit. It should be used flexibly to allow for change as objectives are met and new ones developed. This contract consists of three parts; learning objectives, learning resources and strategies, and evaluation means.

Hamilton and Else have offered some useful suggestions for writing learning contracts which they based on the work of Gronlund.[6] In developing a framework for constructing learning contracts, they note that Gronlund states that the use of specific verbs can provide some clarity in differentiating among goals, objectives, and specific learning activities. For example, goals are concepts with broad, long-term purposes whose attainment cannot be specifically measured.

1. To be an effective group worker.
2. To be an effective programme planner.
3. To be an effective school social worker.

Objectives are framed as specific observable behaviours. Such verbs as; defines, identifies, distinguishes between, interprets, prepares, demonstrates, uses, formulates are examples of verbs which can specify objectives.

1. Demonstrates knowledge of group roles and identifies those roles.
2. Identifies the advantages and disadvantages of a proposed staff training program.
3. Interprets the relevant sections of education legislation to a parent regarding a child with specical needs.

Learning activities are those tasks and situations which are undertaken in order to achieve the learning objectives. Some useful verbs in structuring learning activities are; interview, write, observe, simulate, role play, participate in, accompany, contract, tape, teach, attend, summarize, co-lead.

1. Co-lead a group of recently separated women.
2. Accompany a pupil to a hearing for special placement.
3. Summarize a meeting of agency directors interested in developing programs for seniors.

Setting Learning Objectives

The school will outline overall learning objectives for students in the field practicum. These objectives are likely to define practice in general terms applicable to a variety of practice approaches with a range of clients or projects. The student and field instructor will use these objectives as a framework and relate them to the specific practice of that field setting. The instructor will need to ask what the student needs to learn in this work situation in order to carry a service role. Discussions with the faculty member contracting the practicum and with the student will help determine to what extent the academic curriculum provides the necessary components and to what extent specific knowledge needed will have to be mastered by the student through readings or seminars at the field setting. Students can be helped to explore the preparation they bring from volunteer and work activities, life experiences, and academic courses in order to identify knowledge and skills already developed. Through focusing this discussion on the practicum setting, it may be possible to identify transferable competencies as well as existing gaps. In every practicum three areas can be identified which all students must explore: 1) the agency itself, its structure, policies, procedures, and philosophy; 2) the community, its demography, resources, uniqueness, special problems; 3) the nature of the population served.

Baseline Assessment of Student's Competence

For a contract to be relevant to the student's actual ability it is necessary for the instructor and student to obtain a baseline assessment of the student's competence. It is our conviction that this assessment is meaningful only insofar as it arises out of the student's actual performance. We suggest the following methods to achieve that assessment; observation of the field instructor's practice and observation of the student's practice.

Observation of the field instructor's work should be followed by a discussion focused on the student's observations about the client or target system, the field instructor's interventions, as well as suggestions for continued intervention. In this way field instructors can begin to develop some idea about the student's ability to conceptualize and assess. In addition, field instructors model openness by exposing their own practice to observation, analysis, and critique. As well, they demonstrate the ability to receive feedback.

Observation of the student's work may take place by participating in a session or meeting, observing through a one-way mirror, listening to an audio tape, or watching a video tape. Through discussion about the client or target situation and the student's practice behaviours field instructors will have an opportunity to assess the student's ability to conceptualize and their level of skill. From a few such observation and discussion sequences, field instructors and students will be able to develop specific learning objectives which can then be formalized in a written contract.

The activities of observation, discussion, and objective setting involve the student immediately in integrating theory and practice. Practice behaviours are retrieved and reflected on in relation to meanings, assumptions, and values, and linked to a professional knowledge base in respect to both the client system and the student's skill level. An assessment of the student's skill level specifies the gap between that level and the end goal as a learning objective, a new professional behaviour. We suggest the phase of assessment and goal setting, as in most social work practice models, take place early and the written contract be completed within four to six weeks. It is likely that new learning objectives will be established as the student continues to practice. These objectives should be added to the contract.

Specifying Learning Activities and Resources

The next task is to determine how the learning objectives will be realized. For example, what client, task, or project assignments will the student carry? What educational resources will be available and how will they be structured? Activities such as visits to relevant resources, attendance at seminars, observation of other workers, and relevant readings, may be suggested and arranged.

Since the field instruction relationship is perceived by students as central to their field learning it must be considered as the most important learning resource. In preceding chapters we have discussed various aspects of relationship and its relevance to successful field instruction. In Chapter 3 we presented approaches to field instruction highlighting the variety of models and emphases. In Chapter 4 we presented current concepts regarding preferred learning styles, concluding that all learners present with a variety of learning styles which may be similar to or different from that of their instructor. In Chapter 5 we considered the impact of the fit between learning and teaching styles urging instructors to introduce and discuss these concepts early in the practicum so that a clear understanding of expectations and preferences can be uncovered and a mutual understanding and agreement achieved.

Contracting is a continuing process that provides opportunity to use relationship to encourage growth. Shulman states that field instructors need to clarify purpose, explore the role, reach for feedback from students, and discuss the mutual obligations and expectations regarding the field instructors' authority.[7] He points out that in such a discussion a student may be hesitant to express problems or concerns directly. Instructors need to be sensitive to issues of concern that are hinted at or avoided. In reaching for feedback, instructors will use skills of active listening, and exploration in a supportive, non-judgmental manner to help students participate in the shaping of the field instruction relationship. There are two sensitive areas that should be introduced as soon as possible. The first concerns expectations regarding the mutual responsibility for giving and receiving positive and critical feedback about the student/field instructor working relationship. The second should stress the freedom to make mistakes, to take risks, and to disagree with the field instructor in an open and honest manner.

The process of contracting goes on over time as the implications of these agreeements take on meaning through the activities of daily learning and practice. It is expected that these agreements will be re-discussed, clarified, and perhaps changed in response to such dialogue. Shulman observes that an important way in which the field instructor teaches the contracting skills is by demonstrating them in this context. The student-field instructor contracting process can become a paradigm of the worker-client/project contracting process.

Specifying Evaluation Means

Finally, "who" will evaluate "what" in determining whether the learning objectives are achieved is decided. The field instructor carries primary responsibility for evaluation. It is expected that the student participates fully as well. Other professionals in the setting, the faculty representative, or other field instructors may be involved.

The field instructor and student will decide what data will be used to evaluate progress. Data may include: direct practice data such as observations, audio, or video tape of interviews, meetings, or interactions with colleagues and significant others; indirect practice data such as process records or summary records; documentation prepared in practice such as letters, minutes, summaries, assessments, briefs, proposals, reports; agency information system statistics regarding the number of various activities attended and led; and/or practice outcomes or user satisfaction indicators.

The contract will form the basis for the final evaluation. As well, ongoing feedback and evaluation helps to build the student's confidence and reinforces the acquisition of knowledge and skill. It constitutes a crucial part of the continuous process of contracting. Periodic reviews, at six to eight week intervals may be established to formalize evaluation, or this may be an integral part of field instruction sessions. Evaluations mark the end of each term and are structured by the school. A report and grade is submitted which documents specific aspects of the practicum learning.

Notes

1 Morton L. Arkava and E. Clifford Brennan, eds., *Competency-Based Education for Social Work* (New York: Council on Social Work Education, 1976). A review of field manuals used in Canadian Schools of Social Work revealed general agreement on objectives for field learning.
2 Nina Hamilton and John F. Else, *Designing Field Education: Philosophy, Structure and Process* (Springfield, Illinois: Charles C. Thomas, 1983); Eleanor Hannon Judah, "Responsibilities of the Student in Field Instruction" in *Quality Field Instruction in Social Work*, eds. Bradford W. Sheafor and Lowell E. Jenkins (New York: Longman, 1982), pp. 144-160; Francis Manis, *Openness in Social Work Field Instruction: Stance and Form Guidelines* (California: Kimberly Press, 1979); Lawrence Shulman, *Teaching the Helping Skills: A Field Instructor's Guide* (Illinois: F.E. Peacock, 1983); Suanna J. Wilson, *Field Instruction: Techniques for Supervision* (New York: Macmillan, 1981).

3 Allen Tough, *Why Adults Learn* (Ontario Institute for Studies in Education: Department of Adult Education, 1968).

4 Malcolm Knowles, *Self-Directed Learning* (New York: Association Press, 1975), pp. 14-16; 129-130.

5 David Pratt, "Humanistic Goals and Behavioral Objectives: Toward a Synthesis," *Journal of Curriculum Studies* 8 (1976): 23, quoted in Hamilton and Else, *Designing Field Education.*

6 N.E. Gronlund, *Stating Behavioral Objectives for Classroom Instruction* (New York: Macmillan, 1970) quoted in Hamilton and Else, *Designing Field Education.*

7 Shulman, *Teaching the Helping Skills*, p. 15.

7 Monitoring the Learning Environment

ASSIGNMENTS

Anticipatory anxiety is high for both student and field instructor as the practicum begins. The field instructor who has some case assignments ready for students has taken a step toward anchoring this anxiety.[1] The question of appropriate assignments, however, is always problematic for field instructors. To protect or expose are the horns of the dilemma. Conventional wisdom has directed field instructors to choose assignments carefully so that students would confront relatively uncomplicated situations and would experience initial success. Indeed, in some agencies, cases were labelled as "student" cases and passed on from student to student. These cases usually involved clients with chronic concerns. It is to be hoped that this practice which discouraged both clients and students by perpetuating feelings of powerlessness has fallen into disrepute. Even this practice, however, would sometimes be infused with energy by a student who was capable of taking a fresh look at the situation.

The feeling that students need shelter and an incremental induction into practice situations of increasing complexity is generally pervasive. In reality, the best protected assignment can convert quickly to a complicated situation because of unpredicted events. Matorin queries whether students need such protection and guidance through sequential learning. She wonders whether they might be better equipped to enter the profession by exposure to all kinds of situations.[2] It seems reasonable to accept the fact that such precise sequential assignments are not possible, and more importantly, not useful. Front-line positions are held frequently by beginning workers who need to have had the most demanding student practice experience in regard to complexity and exposure to crisis situations. The protection required by the students can be provided through the careful monitoring of their work so that students feel that immediate guidance and support will keep them afloat no matter what the presenting situation. Supportive instructors have been defined as persons who can tolerate complexity and share with students their own feelings of how difficult it is to work with such complexity both interpersonal and societal. They can acknowledge and own error and encourage students to risk by sharing errors in order to learn from them.[3] The best measure of the range of assignments may be found in the student's expressed interest in the acquisition of new skills.[4]

The number and variety of assignments are more amenable to control than is the factor of complexity. Students differ in their capacity to learn and the speed with which they can assimilate skills. It is almost an aphorism universal to practicum manuals that the school places a premium on education above service as an appropriate guide to student load. Field instructors need to assess the pace which keeps the student busy and progressing but not frenzied or overwhelmed or bored and restless. Some students, through anxiety, want to take on more than can be assimilated while others may be reluctant to undertake assignments because they feel inadequate. Communication which is sensitive and frequent can help field instructors to deal with this anxiety. Evaluation begins with the setting of the learning contract and field instructors need to keep in mind that a range of experiences is important for evaluation of professional competence.

The monitoring process of any assignment can begin by guiding students to identify and acknowledge what they know at the outset that can help them understand a situation and then to discover what they need to learn in addition. This is a variation of partializing, useful to give clients a sense of manageability and also useful to give students a sense of how to approach complexity. It is especially reassuring to tap into already acquired knowledge. For example, applying the ITP loop, a young student anxious about meeting a young woman in hospital with a serious illness which will become chronic was encouraged to think about her own knowledge of life goals of young adulthood, to use her personal experience and her knowledge of developmental theory and the impact of illness to inform her initial approach to her patient. A plan for obtaining additional knowledge and skill needed for effective work can then be developed. Additional knowledge might be greater understanding of the illness, its incidence, etiology, symptoms, treatment and prognosis, interviewing techniques and accurate interpretation, and knowledge of appropriate community resources. A plan to acquire this knowledge and skill might include reading, anticipation and skill development through role playing, observation, and resource searching and contact.

FEEDBACK

Feedback is a term borrowed from rocket engineering by Kurt Lewin, a founder of laboratory education. It has been defined as a "verbal or non-verbal process through which an individual lets others know his perceptions and feelings about his behaviour."[5] It is a critical aspect of field instruction which must be utilized in the service of mutual understanding and is the essential fuel of the ITP loop. That this is so would not be disputed, but feedback, as with the application of any skill, is an art. It can either facilitate learning or retard change.[6] Feedback contains elements of empathy and support but it must provide more than these because in field instruction the purpose is to guide change in the student's knowledge, attitude, or behaviour in a desired direction.[7] Timing is crucial in giving feedback; it has been found that feedback is most effective when it is given immediately after the event.[8]

In her paper on feedback, Freeman discusses many of the following concepts.[9] There is a normal tendency for persons, either student or client, to regress or slow down after an initial success. Feedback can increase the challenge to pursue the change process and can also add important information just when it is most needed. Feedback must be clearly understood, systematic, timely, and reciprocal. It should be based on criteria which are spelled out in advance in behavioural terms. Balanced feedback contains both positive and negative comments though not necessarily in equal portions. In general, presenting feedback in this way makes for greater acceptability. There is no substitute, however, for judgment regarding which students are more sensitive to negative criticism. Students frequently report that they do not know what they are doing right because they never are told by their field instructors. Such students can feel paralyzed by what they perceive as a total attack on their competence to function. These students, in particular, need to be told what they can do well, no matter how slight that accomplishment might be. Balanced feedback is a key concept.

Feedback is seen as more acceptable when the student perceives the field instructor to be qualified and to possess knowledge of the student's concerns derived from direct observation or from information shared by the student. The way the field instructor expresses this concern and expertise is critical. If the student feels that the field instructor comprehends the student's frame of reference, that is, the way the student might view the world, then the chances are good that the student can accept whatever pain the feedback might provoke and work toward change. Additionally, feedback must be reciprocal so that the student feels able to indicate when a message is not understood or is unacceptable. An authoritarian tone taken by the field instructor is not likely to encourage reciprocal feedback and can produce angry silence, compliance, or open resistance.

58

Freeman outlines a four-step plan to ensure optimum learning through feedback.[10] The steps are: 1) clear specification of performance criteria; 2) reliable observation of the student's practice; 3) provision of effective feedback; 4) monitoring the student's use of feedback. The field instructor is cautioned to check on whether the student is getting any conflictual feedback from others, for example, someone from another discipline such as a psychiatrist or psychologist or from the faculty advisor or others in the school. Unless the student can discuss these differing messages openly, the student will be confused and in danger of being drawn into a power struggle. Finally, modelling clear and open feedback for the student will encourage the transfer of this technique to work with clients.

METHODS OF MONITORING

Monitoring the learning environment is the process wherein learning takes place. A wide range of techniques have been developed to help instructors and students with this task. The choice of techniques will depend on many factors such as resource availability, type of practice situation, accountability expectations of the setting, as well as student and instructor preferences. We suggest experimentation with a wide variety of methods so that the instructor and student can develop an effective learning program responsive to the student's learning style and the setting's context.

About Methods Involving Direct Access to Practice Data

...it is not possible to develop practice skills in working with clients or supervision of students without some ongoing means of examining the details of one's practice efforts.[11]

If you are a field instructor in an indirect practice setting we urge you not to skip over this section. While many of the techniques to be discussed have been derived from direct practice, we feel that with imagination they can be adapted to augment field instruction for students in a wide variety of settings. Interpersonal exchanges are a core component of professional social work activity and responsibility for their development must be accepted by both students and field instructors. This means that regardless of setting, students must learn how to engage with others, how to focus, how to listen, and how to resolve conflict so that the desired outcome, ranging from a therapeutic exchange, a community program, or the development of a policy can be achieved. Therefore, the succeeding section will present a summary of the literature on techniques for monitoring and teaching using direct access to practice data. This literature is overly representative of direct practice. The need for reports on the direct access of work from a broader range of settings is apparent. It is important to know what the student is actually doing and saying in community or policy and planning settings.

Numerous studies have demonstrated that students acquire interviewing skills through learning activities that include demonstration, role play, focused use of audio and videotape, feedback, and reinforcement.[12] Barth and Gambrill conducted a study to identify the amount and type of interview training students receive in field learning.[13] They studied chances to observe, to be observed, and to gain feedback as key indicators of training quality. They found that supervisors rarely served as a model of interviewing; supervisors rarely provided feedback on students' performance during actual interviews with clients; and students' interviews with clients were rarely recorded on audiotape or videotape. They concluded:

Trial and error is a slow, frustrating and ineffective instructor. Boosts to interviewing effectiveness are less likely to result from repeated but solitary practice, or even from supervisors' critical responses to after-the-fact reports of interviews, than from specific feedback based on observation of students' performances.[14]

They added that other investigators, Mueller-Lazar and Witkin, demonstrated that modelling plus role-play training resulted in higher skill levels than role play practice alone.[15]

Several reasons are listed in their speculation about the reluctance of field instructors to promote observation, modelling opportunities, and feedback, among which was the fact that this was not the experience of most field instructors during their own social work education. Other factors may be significant such as time and lack of training materials. Time can be utilized in different ways and modelling and role play take no more time than other methods of field instruction that rely more heavily on after-the-fact reports. Direct observation or observing tapes of interviews done by field instructors or other staff can be arranged with the informed consent of clients and assurances about the purpose and use of such observation and taping.

Traditional field instruction consists of discussion of past events and feelings. Rhim notes that conscious and unconscious selection, sifting, and perception will effect what is presented to the instructor.[16] Much of the student's non-verbal behaviour will not be accessible as it may be beyond the student's awareness. The instructor is then faced with the task of "interpreting, commenting upon, and attempting to elicit the underlying meaning based on his assumptions as to what he thinks might have occurred."[17] As actual behaviours of the student and client system are not accessible there may be a tendency to focus on intentions and to attribute meanings not intended.

Some authors note that the use of systems theory has directed attention to the complexity of multiple transactions at various levels of communication.[18] This focus may overwhelm the student in their attempt to keep up with the volume of information evident in any practice situation. Audio and video technology may be a more appropriate media than print to record data based on systemic concepts.

Field instruction based on direct access to an interview or meeting or access to an audio or video record, is more objective and concrete than instruction based on recall. Viewing or hearing the student's actual practice interventions enables an accurate and realistic assessment of learning needs and assists in contracting educational goals and evaluation of goal achievement.

Methods which involve access to actual practice data expose students' work and their immediate emotional reactions. As a result, observation and video taping can be anxiety provoking. This anxiety can be diluted by viewing the work of other students, workers, and the field instructor, with the "mistakes" inherent in any practice endeavour. Seeing experienced practitioners' work, with the normal confusions, repetitions, and even tedium, tends to de-mythologize practice as a logical sequence of activities following a theory and plan. Observation of others' work helps students gain a realistic picture of practice, and may help them become comfortable with "mistakes", and open to risk and learning.

Modelling and/or Observation
Modelling and/or observation requires that the student have the opportunity to observe the field instructor or other staff as they work. Considerable research has shown that a major source of social learning occurs through observing the behaviour of others.[19] Such vicarious learning, framed in an educational context, has been demonstrated to be "an effective, reliable, and rapid technique for the development of new interpersonal responses and the strengthening or weakening of previously acquired social skills."[20] Mayadas and Duehn have concluded from their research, that modelling provides students with more relevant cues than verbal description and facilitates the imitation by students of an array of complex clinical skills while eliminating much trial and error learning inefficiency. They have found that modelling is most effective in teaching affect dimensions of reflection and expression to students who have difficulty with complex interpersonal discrimination.[21]

Other writers reinforce the idea that students most easily acquire skills when these are clearly defined, and when students observe skilled models in action. These skills must be sharpened by practice and students must receive feedback on this practice and suggestions for improvement.[22]

Field instructors have fears about opening their work to the observation of students. It is reassuring to students to learn that there are no perfect interviews and few clearly right or wrong approaches. Human communication is more subtle and complex but purpose and skill can be demonstrated. If students pick up and imitate a phrase or style, no harm is done and what does not "fit" can be discarded as students learn to create their own unique approach. Feedback using the ITP loop is essential and should immediately follow any observation or modelling. Should this occur a new generation of field instructors will emerge who can recall their own training which emphasized both role playing and modelling. In this way, field instruction will have incorporated empirical findings that demonstrate the importance of modelling to learning practice.

Co-working

Co-working is another way to monitor student progress as well as facilitate practice. We define co-working as those instances when the field instructor and the student arrange to share the work, whether it involves an individual, family, group, or project. It is not observation or participant observation, but is an arrangement wherein both field instructor and student play an active role, assessing, planning, and implementing intervention together. The content of field instruction meetings is concerned with joint planning and evaluation and they can be infused with a lively investment of energy. In utilizing the ITP loop, both field instructor and student retrieve the same information but reflection is unique to each. Linkage and planning the professional response becomes a joint effort. Students may sometimes co-work with another staff member but the immediacy of the experience will not be available to the field instructor who will have to depend on feedback from the staff member who is directly involved with the student.

There is a serious reservation that attaches to co-working. Differences in skill level and experience can create an imbalance that can undermine the "co" in co-working. Most writers stress the need for co-therapist egalitarianism as a requisite for a successful group.[23] Indeed, Yalom has stated that use of co-therapists of unequal status was not adviseable under any circumstances.[24] Authority and status of the field instructor in relation to the student reinforce the hierarchy of learner role and instructor role. The inequality of the relationship cannot be denied. However, if the field instructor and student can start from this point but still feel that they can collate their skills and use the experience to enhance the process of learning and teaching, it can be a productive approach for both. It is not an appropriate method for all situations nor all students or field instructors.

The literature contains an interesting report on the use of student and field instructor as group co-therapists.[25] Though the report acknowledges the unequal nature of the relationship, this disadvantage can be overcome by taking steps to build a relationship of mutual acceptance and to build in techniques that will help less experienced students increase their activity. Mutuality is seen as dependent on both student and field instructor developing comfort in exposing their work to comment and evaluation. Students can be encouraged to voice their opinions first in order to minimize their reluctance to disagree with the field insructor. Competitiveness is another concern because it can create problems if the student appears to side with group members in opposition to the field instructor co-therapist. Schlenoff and Busa stress the absolute importance of pre- and post-session discussions where the process can be reviewed utilizing the fact that the process is the live experience of both student and field instructor. Finally, the authors recognize the problem of a student remaining steadfastly resistant to taking a more active role in the group and alternatively, consider the problems created by an overly assertive student. Field instructors might consider that the resistant student's performance anxiety may be related to unclear expectations while the overly assertive student might be encouraged to reflect on the effect he or she may have on the group participants.

Co-worker teams comprised of two students assigned to work with individuals, families, and small groups, have been described in the literature.[26] It was felt that this model facilitated learning co-working approaches and promoted self-awareness.[27] Role playing was utilized by both workers in field instruction sessions and peer learning seemed to produce less defensiveness on the part of the students.[28] Schur cautioned that close supervision was essential and that one had to remain alert to the tendency for the co-working students to reinforce weaknesses particularly in pairs that may have similar gaps in knowledge or similar problems.

Live Supervision
Live supervision is a method of training which has developed in family therapy and training.[29] Using two rooms, separated by a one-way mirror, an instructor, supervisor, or team of experienced workers guides the student or worker while they work directly with a family. Supervision has an immediate impact on the action occurring between student and family. Other students and workers can observe behind the mirror at the same time. Planning and de-briefing sessions can be held before and after the family interview.

This approach assumes that learning is maximized through experiencing the positive effect of successful intervention in a client system. The instructor observes the client situation directly, becoming aware of non-verbal and verbal data, as well as of interactions between family members which may go unnoticed by the student. The instructor does not have to rely on the student's self-report with the selective perception that may accompany that method. Unlike tapes viewed after the event, the observation is simultaneous with the event, providing the opportunity for the instructor to give feedback to the student which can be used to alter the course of intervention with the family. Student and instructor can work specifically on areas identified in contracting. If this method is generally used in the agency students can observe other students and workers during their family interviews and learn from modelling. This model focuses primarily on formulating professional responses. Pre and post-interview sessions can be held to assist students in retrieval of the interview, reflection on the student's experience, and linkage to the knowledge base that led the instructor to suggest particular interventions. If this step is omitted there is the danger of training technicians who remain dependent on co-workers or teams, and are less able to practice autonomously. For students who are observing however, the instructor can highlight phenomena, make linkages to a knowledge base, and discuss a professional response. The challenge, however, still remains to help the student link theory with their own professional behaviours.

The actual communication between student and instructor can occur via telephone, earphone, consultation, or walk-in. Telephone communication consists of phoning into the session delivering a suggestion or message. The information is sent in and received without discussion. If the student is unclear about the directive, clarification can be requested. Short, precise suggestions are most appropriate. As this method is uni-directional, the student cannot respond to the instructor at the time. Consultation occurs when a discussion between the student and instructor takes place and can be initiated by either party. It allows for reciprocal interactions, and some opportunity to briefly discuss proposed interventions. Walk-in refers to the instructor entering a session and leading or participating in the session. This technique may undermine the student's position of responsibility with the family and is used primarily in situations where the client situation requires an immediate therapeutic response that would be too complicated to convey by telephone. The technique chosen depends on the complexity of the intervention, the student's skill level, and the current issue being addressed with the family.

Agencies using this methodology must develop policy and procedures to protect clients' rights for service should they not wish to be observed. Consent forms need to be developed and explained to clients at intake. Some agencies introduce the supervisor and observers to the clients and are explicit in explaining the respective roles of the helpers.

As this is a hierarchical model, it is useful only if students are able to learn through giving up some degree of autonomy and control. It is important that the student and the instructor be able to establish rapport early in their relationship. As well, they must agree on the respective power each has to make decisions about interventions during the client session. They need to agree on the procedures to be used to reach each other during the session. Feedback and monitoring of the supervisory relationship should be a regular feature in this approach. Students report a range of reactions from "being controlled" to "feeling supported."

This model has been developed and used particularly in marital and family therapy. Goodman discusses its use with individual clients.[30] It is also used as a means of monitoring group therapy sessions.

Use of Audio and Video Tape

Technological developments now allow students and field instructors to make use of audio tape and video tape recording and playback in a range of practice situations. Both methods capture the actual client situation and practice behaviours. They do not permit omissions and distortions characteristic of verbal and written reports. Video tape is preferable in that it presents visually the totality of the worker-client system capturing non-verbal communication. As the availability of video taping may be limited due to cost, audio taping is a useful alternative recognizing its limitations.

Using audio or video tape to review one's work allows the student to retrieve actual data easily. It gives field instructors first-hand knowledge of the situation so that they can be more accurate in helping the student form an assessment and intervention plan. One can focus on particular aspects in a session such as interactions between client system members, or interventions of the worker. Students are likely to gain greater awareness of themselves and sensitivity to clients regarding verbal and non-verbal communication which may have been over-looked or misinterpreted.

Students can be helped to reflect on their feelings and thoughts elicited at various parts of a session. They can examine comfort and discomfort with their behaviour and that of the clients. Students become aware of themselves, their motives, sensitivities, and blind spots through the process of viewing or hearing a tape. The field instructor can help the student link practice data to a specific knowledge base. The student's attention can be focused on a set of concepts for organizing perceptions about the data. Professional responses can be identified, labelled, and evaluated. They can be linked to a particular practice model. Alternate responses can be discussed or role played as preparation for future sessions.

Initially, students may feel anxious using audio or video tapes. Star found that an instructor who is open to hearing about student concerns and feels comfortable with the equipment and confident of its usefulness, can create a learning climate that diminishes the anxiety associated with taping.[31] Students tend to relax after using the equipment.

Some agencies have developed a protocol for introducing and explaining taping to clients. The client is asked for permission to tape and informed that taping is voluntary and service will not be withheld should the client deny permission. The client is informed about the technology to be used, specifying that its purpose is for training and supervision. The client is informed about who will hear or observe the tape, and when and how it will be erased. Finally, the client is asked to sign a consent form. If the agency does not have such a protocol the field instructor may wish to use these guidelines to preserve confidentiality and the client's right to service. Involuntary clients in correctional, psychiatric or child welfare agencies may fear the worker's authority and agree to taping but withhold important thoughts, feelings and behaviours as a result. Other clients may be suspicious and fearful of the taping. Professional judgment will help the instructor establish when it is inappropriate to use tapes.

Students may be helped through preparatory role plays to present their request for permission to tape in a comfortable manner. It is sometimes helpful to suggest to a client that the tape be used on a trial basis and discontinued if the client wishes. Students should be instructed to place the machine so that it is visible. They can be assured by the field instructor that both they and the clients will soon ignore its presence. Listening to an entire tape is helpful in obtaining an initial assessment and a final evaluation. For ongoing instruction it is useful to have the student review the tape and analyze it in respect to the ITP loop, reflecting on one's own feelings and thoughts, analyzing practice phenomena and linking it to a knowledge base, and labelling professional responses. Students might be asked to evaluate their interventions and develop alternate responses. The instructor and student can then review and discuss particular segments in the tape.

About Methods Involving Reported Practice Data

Reporting practice events, in written or verbal form, provides the student and instructor with data for field learning. In using these methods one is aware that the actual events are not being reported. Rather the students' perception of those events is conveyed, with all the omissions, distortions, and self-corrections inherent in recalling and describing past events. The instructor is faced with a two-fold task; to determine from the report what might have happened, and to assist the student to reflect about themselves and their practice, make linkages to theory, and plan new professional responses. Reporting, therefore, can be as time consuming as using electronic methods. Methods used for reporting are the process record, summary reports, and verbal reports.

Process Records

Process recording is a written description of the dynamic interactions between a student and persons involved in a social work interaction. Its primary intent is to retrieve the practice experience itself and communicate that experience to the field instructor.

Unlike methods which provide direct access to practice data, process recording allows students the opportunity to control, consciously or unconsciously, what and how much of their practice is included and exposed. In writing, the student may unwittingly impose meanings, structure, or sequences on the data. While distortions and omissions in themselves are revealing, the instructor will be hard pressed to sort out facts from perceptions. Writing process records does provide students with time to recall and reflect on their interviews, the feelings it elicited in them, and the possible effect of their interventions on the client system. Analysis may begin to occur through writing process records.

Generations of social work students have laboriously struggled to recall the details of practice encounters and prepare a process record. Considerable discussion has taken place regarding the inclusiveness of the record. Wilson expects students to communicate everything they can remember, including verbal and non-verbal actions, and their "gut-level" feelings.[32] Urdang also favours total written communication of content as an aid to developing students' ability to recall and reflect on practice.[33] Dwyer and Urbanowski are critical of this detailed approach and argue for structured recording.[34]

Process records are generally submitted to the instructor in advance of the conference with some indication from the student of issues and concerns they would like to discuss. In reading the record the instructor will also note specific areas for discussion. Some instructors go through the entire record, others select segments for discussion, analysis, and possible role play.

Summary Recording

A number of social work educators have been critical of the detailed method of process recording described above.[35] They argue that it does not promote a disciplined and structured approach to practice. Dwyer and Urbanowski developed a structured approach that helps the student record and conceptualize the sessions in terms of purpose, observations, and selected content.[36] The authors suggest that the student include pertinent facts and the responses of client and student to those facts, the feeling content of the session, client preparation for the next interview, and endings. The record should conclude with impressions, student role, and future plans.

Videka-Sherman and Reid point out that a number of summary recording guides have recently been published to address the issue of accountability in social work practice.[37] These guides focus on evaluation of practice intervention, rather than on the occurrences that have taken place during the contact between worker and client. These summary recordings are limited for educational purposes unless they include what the student did and how the client responded.

Videka-Sherman and Reid have developed the Structured Clinical Record, a clinical teaching tool "to assist field instructors to monitor the clinical learning of social work students, and to give the student experience in organizing and reporting on practice which is accountable, systematic, and which links practitioner interventions with client responses."[38] The recording guide consists of face sheet, referral and contextual data; problem formulation; goal statements; and principal interventions. Students are instructed to record their interventions and client responses in specific terms. The goal is to help students reflect on their action and its effect on the client, to determine which interventions are effective and when alternate interventions should be used. The authors state that this form of recording preserves the advantages of process recording by retrieving examples of specific interventions and client responses for consideration.[39] Further, it requires the student to think systematically about the case, linking a generic problem-solving practice theory to intervention and goal attainment. The authors note it has limitations outside of direct practice with the problem-solving model.

Summary recording provides the instructor with students' thinking about their work which has undergone a reformulation. Therefore, actual practice data may be more difficult to retrieve. Recognizing this limitation, the instructor may need to supplement the summary record with verbal inquiries about the practice experience. The instructor will then be able to use the summary record to help students reflect on their practice and their feelings regarding the situation, to link practice phenomena to a knowledge base, and to plan professional responses. The summary recording systems described above provide some direction for the student to begin this work prior to the instructional conference.

Verbal Reports
Verbal reporting of practice situations happens frequently. It is spontaneous, immediate, and may be time saving. The student with good verbal skills may prefer this method to the more time-consuming analysis and writing required by other methods. There is a tendency in verbal reporting to present practice data in an unsystematic fashion rather than engage in more focused retrieval of practice data. Verbal reporting may lead to a consideration of professional responses which may convert field instruction into case management. While this method

may be appropriate in crisis situations, integration of theory and practice necessitates that the practice data presented be subjected to reflection and linkage in forming professional responses.

Group Supervision

Many writers have discussed the usefulness of group supervision as a method for providing field instruction to a group of students.[40] Presenting cases, projects, tasks, and concerns for discussion and instruction to a student group and the field instructor provides students with an opportunity to expand their learning as they hear about assignments other than their own. In this way they are exposed to a wider range of practice situations than that provided by their assignments.

The group medium can provide significant affective learning if students are encouraged to express and work on emotional concerns connected with learning to practice.[41] The instructor can help students express and identify the various issues or conflicts characteristic of student learning, for example, feelings of inadequacy, fear, being overwhelmed, concern with professionalism, use of authority and social control, and self-determination. Emotional support is experienced as students perceive their peers struggling with similar feelings. The instructor can encourage reflection and expression of each student's own unique ways of understanding and responding to these issues. Students will become aware of a range of potential responses to the same problem. Through clarification of their own feelings and attitudes students can work on developing relatively unconflicted approaches to practice issues.

Student groups offer an opportunity to link specific knowledge to client or project concerns. The instructor may provide the knowledge base or draw on group members to present appropriate readings. The small group provides the opportunity for active participation in analyzing, discussing, and linking the concepts to particularly real situations facing the students. Knowledge necessary for all students to learn in a specific field setting can be structured so as to complement field experiences. For example, students in a setting serving non-voluntary clients can have a group session providing a conceptual base for engagement with this client group; students embarking on a community action project to change housing by-laws can learn about significant legislation in a group presentation.

New practice responses can be formulated and rehearsed through role play until the student feels comfortable enough to transfer new learning to the actual practice situation. Peers as well as the field instructor can provide feedback as students attempt to master new behaviours.

The literature notes that the effective functioning of the learning group is dependent on the expectations and patterns of interaction that develop in a particular group.[42] Knowledge of group dynamics and skill in group practice, enables the field instructor to focus the group process productively. Field instructors are cautioned to be aware that some groups may become too introspective and overly focused on self-awareness while others may avoid dealing with affect and focus exclusively on case management. Some group members may engage in competition and rivalry in respect to the authority of the field instructor. Cowan et al note that students valued group learning for understanding general social work concepts, but needed individual sessions as well for questions they considered important for their own learning.[43]

Role Play
It is an aphorism that all the world is a stage. Because this is so, field instructors and students can join in holding "a mirror up to nature" in order to replay or rehearse the feel of a real situation. The "as if" nature of this technique ensures a feeling of safety and permits the student to risk, to try out, to play out an idea.

Role play can be either anticipatory or a replay of a past occurrence. It can be utilized when the field instructor and student wish either to experience actively the retrieval of a part of an interview that has already occurred or to anticipate a responsive exchange. They can try on possible ways to develop a theme or cope with an expected or unexpected response. Role play can also be effective in that part of the reflective phase of the ITP loop when student and field instructor search for answers to why a particular strategy was not successful. Role play permits the rehearsal of a specific skill which may have been identified as a learning objective, such as the use of open questions, or focussing, or confronting a client around a specific concern. The field instructor may assume the client's role or that of the worker with the student as the client. The assumption of the client role can provide the student with an expanded perspective of the world as the client perceives it. Role play is an indispensible tool limited only by the field instructor's imagination. For the field instructor and student who learn best by active experimentation and concrete experience, it is an important technique.

ON WRITING SKILLS

Writing is an aspect of the practicum that is frequently neglected. This is surprising, since the importance of good writing ability is obvious in order to meet the demand for concise, informative assessments, court reports, hospital chart notes, special program designs, project reports, policy statements, personnel practice policy, training manuals, and professional letters.

It must be admitted that students and field instructors as well vary widely in the ability to spell, to construct proper sentences, and to

RETRIEVAL	REFLECTION	LINKAGE	PROFESSIONAL RESPONSE
Observation Co-working Live supervision Audio Tape Video Tape Process Record Summary Record Verbal Report	1. Start with the student's life experience associations 2. Identify the student's feelings, thoughts, assumptions regarding the practice data 3. Identify and label the student's practive behaviour and its effect on the client system 4. Give feedback regarding the student's behaviour. Feedback should be: a. Empathetic b. Timely c. Clear and direct d. Systematic e. Reciprocal f. Based on criteria expressed in the learning objectives and stated in behavioural terms	1. Start with the student's cognitive associations eliciting their rationale, and understanding of this behaviour 2. Give your own cognitive associations. Identify the theoretical concepts you are using to explain, examine, and analyze client practice phenomena 3. Encourage the student to look for the fit or lack of fit between the the theory and the specific practice situation 4. Use relevant theories to form a new pro-fessional response	Discuss alternate responses. Model Role Play Co-working Live supervision

organize thoughts and information expressed in writing. Learning to write well, whatever is required by a particular agency or particular setting, should be a primary goal of all field instructors for every student.

Writing is a requisite skill of every university program, however, researching and writing papers for courses does not seem to provide adequate preparation for the special skills required for professional writing of the kind listed above. These skills include selection of relevant data based on the purpose of the document, report, record, or letter, some knowledge of who will read it which should inform what is to be included, and ability to synthesize the information so that it appears organized, logical, and clear.

Most agencies attempt to facilitate the organization of assessments by providing an outline form of the required information. If such a form is not available, field instructors should develop an outline together with the student. Modelling can be helpful by making available to the student sample assessments, reports, or letters that have been written by others in order to give the student an idea of composition, form, and style.

It is strongly recommended that learning objectives include practicing professional writing skill and that specific learning activities should include writing a particular kind of report or record required of workers in that setting.

Notes

1 Nancy Webb, "Developing Competent Clinical Practitioners: A Model With Guidelines for Supervisors," *The Clinical Supervisor* 4 (Spring 1983): 46.
2 Susan Matorin, "Dimensions of Student Supervision: A Point of View," *Social Casework* 60 (March 1979): 150–156.
3 Ibid.
4 Zvi Eisikovits and Edna Guttman, "Toward a Practice Theory of Learning Through Experience in Social Work Supervision," *The Clinical Supervisor* 1 (Spring 1983): 51–63.
5 Phillip B. Hanson, "Giving Feedback: An Interpersonal Skill," *The 1975 Annual Handbook for Group Facilitators*, p. 147.
6 Edith M. Freeman, "The Importance of Feedback in Clinical Supervision: Implications for Direct Practice," *The Clinical Supervisor* 3 (Spring 1985): 5.
7 Ibid., p. 6.
8 Ibid., p. 8; Also see Hanson, "Giving Feedback: An Interpersonal Skill," p. 8; and A.E. Kazdin, *The Token Economy* (New York: Plenum, 1977).
9 Ibid., pp. 8–21.
10 Ibid., p. 14.
11 Lawrence Shulman, *Teaching the Helping Skills:A Field Instructor's Guide* (Itasca, Illinois: F.E. Peacock, 1983), p. 14.

12 Donald Collins and Marion Bogo, "Competency-Based Field Instruction: Bridging the Gap Between Laboratory and Field Learning," *The Clinical Supervisor*, forthcoming; Judith Magill and Annette Werk, "Classroom Training as Preparation for the Social Work Practicum: An Evaluation of a Skills Laboratory Training Program," *The Clinical Supervisor* 3 (Fall 1985): 69–76; Nazneen S. Mayadas and Wayne D. Duehn, "The Effects of Training Formats and Interpersonal Discriminations in the Education for Clinical Social Work Practice," *Journal of Social Service Research* 1 (Winter 1977): 208–13; Barbara Star, "Exploring the Boundaries of Videotape Self-Confrontation," *Journal of Education for Social Work* 15 (Winter 1979): 87–94.

13 Richard P. Barth and Eileen D. Gambrill, "Learning to Interview: The Quality of Training Opportunities," *The Clinical Supervisor* 2 (Spring 1984): 3–14.

14 Ibid., p. 9.

15 Ibid., p. 5.

16 Bonnie C. Rhim, "The Use of Videotapes in Social Work Agencies," *Social Casework* 57 (December 1976): 644.

17 Ibid., p. 644.

18 Rae Meltzer, "School and Agency Co-operation in Using Videotape in Social Work Education," *Journal of Education for Social Work* 13 (Winter 1977): 90; Rhim, "The Use of Videotapes in Social Work Agencies", p. 646.

19 A. Bandura, *Principles of Behavior Modification* (New York: Holt, Rinehart and Winston, 1969).

20 Mayadas and Duehn, "The Effects of Training Formats and Interpersonal Discrimination in the Education for Clinical Social Work Practice," p. 149.

21 Ibid., p. 157.

22 Barth and Gambrill, "Learning to Interview: The Quality of Training Opportunities." The authors cite Bandura, 1977, Gagne, 1977, and Morton and Kurtz, 1980, all of whom made similar findings.

23 Marjorie Litwin Schlenoff and Sandra Hricko Busa, "Student and Field Instructor as Group Co-Therapists: Equalizing an Unequal Relationship," *Journal of Education for Social Work* 17 (Winter 1981): 29–35.

24 J. Yalom, *The Theory and Practice of Group Psychotherapy* (New York: Basic Books, 1969).

25 Schlenoff and Busa, "Student and Field Instructor as Group Co-Therapists: Equalizing an Unequal Relationship," pp. 29–35.

26 Edith L. Schur, "The Use of the Co-Worker Approach as a Teaching Model in Graduate Field Education," *Journal of Education for Social Work* 15 (Winter 1979): 72–79.

27 Ibid., p. 74.

28 Ibid., p. 78.

29 Vernon C. Rickert and John C. Turner, "Through the Looking Glass: Supervision in Family Therapy," *Social Casework* 59 (March 1978): 131–137 are the only authors who discuss the use of this approach specifically with social

work students. The following authors present a full description and discussion of this technique in training family therapists from a variety of disciplines: Michael Berger and Carrell Dammann, "Live Supervision as Context, Treatment, and Training," *Family Process* 21 (September 1982): 337–344; Howard A. Liddle and Richard C. Schwartz , "Live Supervision/ Consultation: Conceptual and Pragmatic Guidelines for Family Therapy Trainers," *Family Process* 22 (December 1983): 477–490; Braulio Montalvo, "Aspects of Live Supervision," *Family Process* 12 (December 1973): 343–60.

30 Ronald W. Goodman, "The Live Supervision Model in Clinical Training," *The Clinical Supervisor* 3 (Summer 1985): 43–49.

31 Barbara Star, "Exploring the Boundaries of Videotape Self- Confrontation," p. 91.

32 Suanna J. Wilson, *Field Instruction: Techniques for Supervision* (New York: Macmillan, 1981), p. 118.

33 Esther Urdang, "On Defense of Process Recording," *Smith College Studies in Social Work* 50 (November 1979): 1–15.

34 Margaret Dwyer and Martha Urbanowski, "Student Process Recording: A Plea for Structure," *Social Casework* 46 (May 1965): 282–286.

35 Ibid.; E. Clifford Brennan, "Evaluation of Field Teaching and Learning," in *Quality Field Instruction in Social Work*, eds. Bradford W. Sheafor and Lowell E. Jenkins (New York: Longman, 1982), pp. 76–97.

36 Dwyer and Urbanowski, "Student Process Recording: A Plea for Structure," pp. 283–286.

37 Lynn Videka-Sherman and William J. Reid, "The Structured Clinical Record: A Clinical Education Tool," *The Clinical Supervisor* 3 (Spring 1985): 45–62.

38 Ibid., p. 47.

39 Ibid., p. 60.

40 Paul Abels, "Group Supervision of Students and Staff," in *Supervision, Consultation, and Staff Training in the Helping Professions*, ed. Florence W. Kaslow (San Francisco, California: Jossey-Bass, 1977), 175–198; Barbara Cowan, Rose Dastyk and Edcil R. Wickham, "Group Supervision as a Teaching/Learning Modality in Social Work," *The Social Worker/Le Travailleur Social* 40 (4 1972): 256–261; Friedericka Mayers, "Differential Use of Group Teaching in First Year Field Work," *Social Service Review* 44 (March 1970): 63–70; Lawrence Shulman, *Skills of Supervision and Staff Management* (Itasca, Illinois: F.E. Peacock, 1982).

41 Friedericka Mayers, "Differential Use of Group Teaching in First Year Field Work," pp. 69–70.

42 Paul Abels, "Group Supervision of Students and Staff"; Barbara Cowan, Rose Dastyk, and Edcil R. Wickham, "Group Supervision as a Teaching/Learning Modality in Social Work," pp. 256–261.

43 Ibid., p. 260.

Special Situations

This chapter will explore specific characteristics of students who differ in significant ways from the average or normative type of student. These special situations can be troublesome or difficult for the field instructor, the student, and the school. Some anticipation, therefore, can serve to facilitate preparation and planning in order to minimize the strains and to provide an optimum practice experience.

THE EXCEPTIONALLY GOOD STUDENT

The exceptionally good student possesses competence beyond our general expectation of a student at a particular level of education. This student may be naturally suited to social work and possess strong interpersonal skills, good organizational abilities, a critical and lively intellect, and strong commitment to helping. The good student already possesses skills, appears trustworthy, and is able to practice with little help from the instructor. This student can relate theory to practice and may present the instructor with completed work of a high quality.

Instructors may experience a range of sentiments, from challenge to threat, when faced with the extremely competent student. The instructor may question what they have to teach such a student and be concerned that they may not be able to provide the student with enough stimulation or challenge. There may be a tendency for the instructor and others in the setting to see such a student as a colleague and expect them to function as a trained worker. They may then avoid giving the student opportunities to ask questions, flounder, or "be taught". Exceptionally good students often have a history of others expecting them to function well and independently. They may accept this collegial relationship and not request the intensive teaching expected in field instruction. Instructors might be so pleased with the student's performance that they may not challenge the student enough in setting learning objectives, practice assignments, or issues raised in instruction.

Exceptionally good students may have difficulty admitting that they do not know something and need some assistance from their field instructor. Accustomed to being competent and knowing, the state of not knowing may be experienced as uncomfortable. The student may struggle alone in attempting to maintain their sense of self as a competent person. This student needs an instructor who will reach for the student's concerns regarding practice issues and their own expectations about themselves as a learner. The instructor may need to give permission to the student to be less than perfect, to risk, and to make mistakes.

Exceptionally good students may adopt a variety of positions in a student group. In some instances such students will attempt to be extremely helpful to their peers and give them assistance and advice about their practice assignments. The role of helper to other students may undercut the natural competitiveness and envy that students in a unit may experience towards the good student. In other instances, the star student may be openly critical of peers' practice efforts, give negative feedback frequently and heighten competitive tensions in the group. Or, good students may choose to avoid standing out as special amongst their peers, withholding their thoughts and limiting their participation in the group sessions. Field instructors comfortable with group work will handle these situations within the group while others will address these issues in individual conferences. What is important is that the students develop sensitivity to the effect of their attitudes and behaviour on others.

THE MARGINAL OR FAILING STUDENT

The possession of a social work degree credits a graduate as a competent social work practitioner. Though some jurisdictions have enacted legislation regulating social work practice, for the most part, the schools of social work are the gatekeepers controlling entry into the profession. Most students admitted into a university program possess the necessary scholastic aptitude to sucessfully complete academic courses. This does not necessarily mean that they are suited for professional practice. Therefore the field instructor may be the first person to identify students who are not able to learn competent social work practice.

Social workers are trained to help, and believe in the potential for individuals to grow, develop, and change. When confronted with problematic behaviours on the part of a student this orientation is likely to prevail. Instructors tend to view problematic behaviour with equanimity, almost expecting lack of competence as typical of beginning students. They will encourage identification of issues and expect students to progress and regress, to struggle and accept, as they engage in learning in the field setting. However, when students are consistently unable to demonstrate enough learning through changed behaviour then the instructor must consider recommending a failing grade.

Wilson notes that field instructors find it difficult to fail students.[1] Regardless of their level of experience instructors tend to doubt themselves, questioning whether a student's failure is attributable to them. They may feel they were unable to teach the student due to differences in style, personality clashes, the nature of the practice assignments, the amount of time they gave, or the approaches they used. They may also question their own standards and wonder if their expectations are too high and whether another instructor would pass the student. They wonder if the faculty representative will support them or see them as unrealistic in their expectations.

Some instructors may have had equivocal experiences with their own field instructors, with supervisors, or with the particular school. This may lead to over-identification with the student and a wish to protect or rescue the student, resulting in a collusion to keep the faculty representative uninformed about a failing performance.

Students will react to failing evaluations in a variety of ways. While some will agree with the evaluation, others may be quite upset and verbally hostile requiring field instructors to deal with considerable conflict. Failing grades are often challenged by students in grievance or appeal hearings. Most often the student's case rests on a critique of the field instruction. It takes strength, conviction, and commitment to standards for an instructor to take a stand regarding failure.

Importance of Documentation

Firm evidence must be available to substantiate the decision that a student does not meet the objectives of the program. A recent survey in one Canadian school regarding field instructors' reluctance to fail students found that the major reason for not failing a student is lack of firm evidence.[2] Schools provide objectives for the practicum which the instructor and student concretize and individualize through the mechanism of contracting. The learning contract specifies the learning resources to be used to help the student meet those objectives, and the evidence to be examined to evaluate whether the learning objectives have been attained. Discussions and decisions about passing or failing takes place within this framework.

When a field instructor has concerns about a student's performance these concerns should be documented and shared with the student as soon as possible. In general, this should occur before or at the mid-way point. Evidence to substantiate the concern should be available such as taped interviews, process records, reports, memos, notes from instructional sessions summarizing issues discussed and student responses.

The faculty representative should be consulted. Schools have procedures regarding the failing student which should be followed. The faculty representative can clarify the expectations of student performance and the degree to which the particular student is at risk of failing. Some schools have provided opportunities for field instructors to meet together to assess the performance of students in difficulty. The faculty representative can also help the student and instructor evaluate their field instruction sessions in regard to learning style needs, frequency of sessions, and whether feedback has been specific, frequent, and understood.

The early identification of learning issues can help the instructor and student set concrete, clear, behavioural objectives for the student at risk. Re-contracting may take place at this point specifying the time frame for the achievement of certain behaviours and the evidence to be used to assess progress. This provides the student with the opportunity to demonstrate change. It is useful for the field instructor to keep notes of the field instruction sessions highlighting issues discussed and responses to feedback. Field instructors must enlist the active involvement of the faculty representative to monitor the progress of a student in danger of failing. These reviews should be documented so that all partners are fully aware of concerns and plans. Though this structure may help the student to achieve a passing grade this is not always possible. For some students, there is no way to prevent failure. The steps suggested above, however, should prepare the student for a negative evaluation and a recommendation to the school of a failing grade.

Students who are at risk of failing are likely to experience considerable anxiety about their performance. They may become so overwhelmed by their fear of failure that they become unable to learn. It is helpful to discuss these feelings, and offer realistic support and encouragement. Focusing on the process of learning and the changed behaviour expected may help the student partialize the task and reduce anxiety.

Indicators

Indicators of Problems in Learning Practice

Students fail the practicum because of the presence of dysfunctional behaviours which are inappropriate for the professional practice of social work, or because they have not been able to develop competence in professional practice, or any significant combination of the above. It is not sufficient to state that students can pass because they will do no harm. Incompetent service given to a client in need is as harmful as a worker who is actively destructive. The presence of the indicators discussed here should alert field instructors to the existence of potential problems. These should be raised with the student and if a satisfactory resolution can not be found field instructors should request the involvement of the faculty representative.

A number of dysfunctional behaviours have been associated with unsatisfactory performance.[3] The student who displays behaviours which are destructive to others, and which are clearly unprofessional, must be removed from the practicum setting. Examples would be physically injuring someone, appearing at the agency intoxicated or drugged, having frequent temper outbursts, sexually seducing clients, stealing, threatening to harm clients, staff, other students, or the instructor. Such behaviour may indicate mental illness or extreme personality disorders. When confronted with their behaviour, students may deny that it has occurred and blame the instructor for causing the student difficulty with the school. In these situations the instructor and faculty representative must use their professional judgment and terminate the practicum if clients and others are at risk. Appropriate educational review procedures should be used in such extreme situations.

Some dysfunctional behaviours may be sporadic leaving the instructor with concerns about the student's capacity to learn and perform appropriately. Examples are inconsistent attendance or lateness, or periodic lying about work done. While not as obviously indicative of personality problems as the earlier examples, the instructor will be left feeling uncertain about the student's honesty, trustworthiness, and readiness to learn. In such situations concerns should be documented and brought to the student's attention. The faculty representative should be involved to help clarify appropriate expected behaviours and to determine whether the student is to continue in the setting.

For most students who fail the practicum difficulties in learning will be expressed in practice with clients or project assignments. Evidence, on audio or video tape, in written records or reports, or in memos describing the behaviour must be available which demonstrate persistent problem areas. In general, students who fail have difficulty using social work theory in respect to purpose, role, function, and process to guide their behaviour in the practice assignments. They cannot develop purposeful collaborative relationships with clients or user groups that enables participation in assessment, planning, intervention, and evaluation of service. Some of the specific problems in this regard are discussed below. Most students manifest many of these behaviours early in the practicum. Field instructors should become concerned if these behaviours persist after they have directed the student's attention to their repeated use.

Some students have strong beliefs or values which they impose on their clients with conviction. They cannot accept the social work value of a non-judgmental, respectful attitude. They tend to be tenacious and dogmatic in their belief system and attempt to convince the client to see things their way. They may be judgmental and critical of the client, harsh, angry, bullying, or subtly depreciating and condescending.

Students need to develop an appropriate stance between direction and non-direction. Students who are overly authoritarian, directive, and task-oriented may have difficulty forming a working relationship with the client based on mutuality. Their interaction may be cold, aloof, business like. They may prescribe behaviour inappropriate to their client's needs. They may tend to lecture to clients trying to convince them to adopt the student's plan. At the other extreme is the student who is unable to provide appropriate leadership and direction to the social work purpose. This student may be shy, ill at ease, overwhelmed by being a professional. These feelings may be seen in a lack of appropriate eye contact, uncomfortable and distancing body posture, a frightened or quiet voice tone, a tendency to be silent too often, as well as the absence of behaviours which focus the practice task.

A number of problematic behaviours arise from students who over-personalize their professional activity. Such students are extremely preoccupied with themselves, their feelings, and their needs to feel comfortable. Mishne notes that many social work students are struggling with their own self-esteem and their needs to be liked and successful.[4] The complexities and uncertainties of social work theory and practice create a conflict with these needs. This conflict will be seen in inappropriate reactions while delivering service, such as shock or disbelief regarding clients' life styles and choices, attempts to get clients to like the student, anger at clients, groups, or committees who do not comply with the student's wishes, inability to listen to client messages as students attempt to do something for their clients to reduce their own sense of helplessness, and refusal to work with client groups who make them feel uncomfortable or upset.

Some students equate professional behaviour with a cold, aloof stance. They feel they must reject this stereotype by adopting a natural, spontaneous, and friendly relationship with the client. Self-disclosure is used inappropriately to meet the student's need for comfort and the client is burdened with listening to the student's problems.

Some students have difficulty dealing with conflict, and, uncertain about how to handle it, react by keeping their practice at a superficial level. They may engage in social conversations, not respond to negatives or conflict when these are brought up by the client, change the subject to a less conflictual one, and avoid clarifying underlying negative dynamics. Such students may actually avoid face-to-face contacts and report few meetings with clients or user groups.

Indicators of Problems in Organizational Behaviour and Professional Collaboration
All settings have policies, regulations, and practices which apply to

students as well as staff. Though students should appropriately question organizational policy and practice, the failing student will unilaterally contravene agency policy, without first raising concerns with the field instructor.

Professional staff from other disciplines may find the failing student unwilling or unable to collaborate on behalf of the client. The student may seem mistrustful by withholding important information or by being destructively critical of other staff to the client. The student may behave inappropriately with other professional staff, treating them in a depreciating manner, giving orders, or embarrassing them in team meetings.

Students need to learn to give feedback to others that will be accepted and used. It is expected that in learning these skills students may be too passive or too aggressive. It is also expected that students use field instruction to retrieve these situations, and reflect on the impact of their behaviours on others. Failing students are unable to appreciate the effect of their actions and continue to repeat them despite considerable discussion in field instruction.

Indicators of Problems in The Use of Field Instruction

Students who demonstrate problematic behaviours in practice and in collaboration with other staff generally have difficulty in using field instruction productively. Failing students often do not understand what social work theory and practice actually mean. These students may know theory presented in academic courses, however, they cannot use these concepts in their practice. They rely heavily on the instructor to tell them what to do. They do not necessarily learn from the concrete experience. Each situation feels new and they ask repeatedly for the same direction and structure. Incremental gains in learning are not seen. Confusion and mistakes appear again and again.

Some students, for a variety of personal reasons related to trust and risk, cannot be open with their field instructor. They avoid exposing their behaviour in practice situations, they do not ask for help with issues they are uncertain about, they do not admit to mistakes or problems. These students are usually very uncomfortable in any discussion about their own reactions and may respond with silence or cautious minimal comments. As they cannot engage in discussion about what is happening to them, they are greatly hindered in developing self-awareness and tend to act without adequate reflection.

Some students attempt to use field instruction for personal therapy bringing their problems to instruction and seeking help. Field instructors may notice that these students are overly concerned about their own reactions in a professional exchange and tend to omit any reflection of how others may be feeling.

Some students overly personalize feedback and experience it as a validation of or an attack on their self esteem and personal worth. They may focus considerable attention on trying to please the instructor, always agreeing with the feedback, but not changing in any significant way. Alternatively, a tenuous sense of self-worth may permit only negative feedback to be heard while positive comments are screened. Students can become so concerned with the quality of their performance, that they have difficulty connecting to the needs of the practice situation. They can become immobilized and unable to learn.

Students who experience negative feedback as a blow to their self esteem may not hear what the instructor is saying. Their energy may go into defending their actions with explanations, blaming others or the situation for their lack of competence. Such students at some point may project blame for their poor performance onto the field instructor. Some recriminations expressed by students include personality incompatibility, insufficient support and direction, allegations of bias or discrimination, and unrealistic expectations of the student. These negative perceptions may be indicative of a failing student or may be an accurate reflection of the interaction between student and field instructor. When serious disagreements cannnot be resolved the faculty representative should be alerted as soon as possible. The school has a responsibility to assist both student and field instructor to mediate and seek a fair solution to problems.

THE RESISTANT STUDENT

The resistant student is different from the marginal or failing student. This is the student who gives evidence of competence and knowledge but who seems intent upon keeping the field instructor at arms length. It seems as if the goal is to avoid engaging with the field instructor because to do so is to risk exposure. The resistant student is certainly manifesting performance anxiety but the student contains the anxiety with a facade of competence. It is a defensive armour that is difficult for the field instructor to dent.

In a classic article, Kadushin comments that "the supervisory situation generates a number of different kinds of anxieties for the supervisee".[5] Kadushin believes that this anxiety is generated by the field experience because of the expectation that the student must make changes in behaviour and in some cases in personality. The demand for change threatens long-standing patterns of thinking and believing and may be perceived as a betrayal of earlier role models, teachers and peers, whose behaviour and beliefs have been incorporated but which may now need to be re-examined.[6]

Three examples of the resistant student can be developed in which the competence base is the variable. The first is the student who is fearful about possessing no theory of practice and few skills and fears that this utter lack of competence will be revealed. This student handles rising panic by attempting to avoid all direct exposure of his work.

The second example is the student who is comfortable with a minimal level of competence, using a pleasant personality that lends itself to easy relationships. This student may try to ward off any pressure to move beyond this level of professional functioning. The student is afraid to let go of "niceness" and easy acceptance and resists the demand for more substantive analysis and goal-directed performance. It is easy for such a student to collude with clients who are also ambivalent about the demand for change and movement.

The third example is the student who does not accept the learner role and wishes to operate quite independently of the field instructor. Case management decisions, for example, may be readily discussed, but there is reluctance to focus on the student's part in transactions.

Field instructors can turn to the ITP loop to help such students recogize the resistant nature of their behaviour. Building on the initial working contract of mutual expectations and responsibilities, field instructors can identify their strong feelings that resistance to the learning contract is being demonstrated by the student through what is brought to instruction sessions and what is omitted. Field instructors can then retrieve the facts of the field instruction sessions and reflect on the incompleteness of the facts and the frustration this is producing because learning and teaching is inhibited. Anxiety arising from the perceived danger of exposure of incompetence and the wish to avoid the pain of incorporating behavioural and conceptual change can be described and linked to learning theory. The theoretical linkage can be reassuring in that what the student is feeling is commonly experienced by learners. The general discussion of the student's resistance to the terms of the learning contract may lead to facilitating a new response to field instruction on the part of the student.

THE MATURE STUDENT

The mature student is not uncommon in social work education. This student may have come late to post-secondary education after work experience in a field unrelated to social work or may have waited until family responsibilities lessened before returning to school. Some mature students have worked in social work settings as social workers before entering a degree program. These students can present difficulty to field instructors.

In general, mature students are apprehensive about entering university well beyond the usual age of entry. They are concerned about their capacity to study, to integrate new knowledge, and to refute the caveat that "you can't teach an old dog new tricks." They may feel that younger students and faculty will expect them to possess knowledge just because they have been around longer or that younger students will laugh at them. Whatever the combination of fears, it must be accepted that they feel somewhat uneasy about assuming the student role.

The mature student who enters the social work practicum with work experience in a field unrelated to social work has made a significant career change. This student may have been quite competent in the former work role and now feels like a "rookie" confronting an unknown set of expectations and skills. The field instructor may be younger than the student and this fact may increase the initial discomfort of both student and field instructor. The field instructor must initiate discussion of the mature student's concerns and thoughts about being a student in a social work setting, undertaking social work assignments and being expected to submit their work to the scrutiny of the field instructor. It is helpful to acknowledge the value of the mature student's life experience and employment experience in another field. It is important to encourage the student to draw upon aspects of that experience that are relevant to the current situation, both from an organizational point of view and in regard to the social problems addressed by that agency. This process should be an ongoing one as the student begins to develop assignments and to work with clients. The field instructor must help the student to keep a balance between the use of maturity and experience and the need to suspend old and fixed ideas that may stand in the way of growth and learning.

The mature student who has worked in a social work setting before entering a social work degree program presents a different challenge to the field instructor. This student may resent the student role, may feel equally competent or more competent than the field instructor. Alternately, some students in this position, want to deny their experience and may tend to belittle or downgrade their knowledge and experience in order to be a student just like anyone else. In reality, some of these students are comfortable with the worker role, do understand organizational structure and may possess real competence with clients and social work process. However, some may bring with them a narrow and punitive attitude toward clients and social work process because of having worked with inadequate resources and heavy caseloads as front-line workers. On the other hand, students with the same work experience may have developed a strong commitment to social work values.

It is important for the field instructor to acknowledge the student's experience and to suggest that they work together to establish the base level of competence possessed by the student at the outset of the practicum. It is then possible to negotiate what learning goals should be set that will provide a challenge for new learning during the practicum. Students may believe that they possess greater or lesser competence than is actually the case. Either discrepancy must be addressed and resolved if real work is to take place. One must guard against the seductive pull of settling into a comfortable collegial relationship in which no real growth is expected or promoted.

For some students, a career change may create problems for both the student and the field instructor. Frames of reference and practiced patterns of behaviour are difficult to shift when the student enters a working environment through the practicum. Former careers and professional experience in nursing, teaching, or fields such as commercial public relations may create conflict as the student struggles to define the differences and similarities in the approach to persons from a social work perspective.

Nursing and teaching provide far more structured professional behaviour in which performance anxiety may be contained. Routines and procedures can be learned and repeated from situation to situation and as competence develops anxiety diminishes. Social work approaches do not include detailed lesson plans or medical procedures but rather emphasize a stance that is open to the perception and utilization of feelings and thoughts present in the ongoing interchange beween worker and others.

If field instructors are not aware that students may have difficulty with the differences in professional approach, the discomfort, confusion and mounting anxiety can threaten the student-field instructor relationship and the practicum itself. If these differences can be recognized, both the student and field instructor can be relieved of the personal struggle and can focus energy on helping the student to separate past professional behaviour from the requirements of the current social work task.

THE HANDICAPPED STUDENT

The physically handicapped student can present a special situation for the practicum field instructor. Though social work programs admit and graduate students with a variety of physical handicaps, professional literature has said little about the practicum aspect of their education.*

The most common physical problems include motor disabilities which may require a wheelchair for mobility and auditory or visual defects ranging from moderate impairment to profound deafness or blindness. In general, most universities have accommodated to permit physically

---

*We wish to thank Barbara Edwardes-Evans, Chief Social Worker, Co-ordinator, Deafness Clinic, Clarke Institute of Psychiatry, Toronto, Ontario. Ms. Edwardes-Evans has been a field instructor for handicapped students and graciously shared her observations with us.

handicapped students to move about the campus and to have access to most classrooms. Special assistance in the form of readers, attendants, interpreters, Braille texts, and special electronic equipment have made it possible for students to keep up with classroom work. Difficulties may arise, however, when the handicapped student must move away from the campus and into the community. These students face the community daily and are well aware of what they require to facilitate functioning. Entry into a student-professional worker role, however, may create new anxiety. Preparation of the field instructor by the faculty representative is essential in paving the way for a handicapped student. Careful planning is required so that specific adjustments can be made to create an environment in which the student can function. Preparation of other staff should precede the arrival of the student and continue throughout the practicum. This is essential because unless the concerns and observations of others are considered promptly and resolved, the student and the practicum can be adversely affected. For example, other workers may be reluctant to assign cases to the student unless their fears can be addressed.

The more complex issues are the psychological ones. Although all students approach the practicum with heightened concern regarding how well they will be accepted, for the handicapped student, this acceptance factor is critical. For the initial interview, the field instructor must be prepared to look beyond the handicap and to consider the whole student. Handicapped students are comprised of much more than their handicap; that is, they bring skills, personal attitudes, and life goals to the same degree as any student. Their handicap, however, is also a fact of that person's life. Field instructors should be wary if the student does not address specific adjustments and needs relevant to their disability, or if the disability becomes the sole focus of the interview. Student learning needs and the expectations of the university and the agency remain constant. The fact of a disability must not be used by either the student or the field instructor as a reason to go easy, to shrink from making demands for learning, developing professional behaviour, and adhering to agency procedure. Adjustments in regard to time needs and assignments, if they are required, must be disability specific; for example, if the disability means that more time is required to get from place to place, or if the student is dependent on special transportation, then work assignments should be adjusted accordingly.

The formulation of a learning contract is of particular importance for the handicapped student. Through developing a learning contract, both field instructor and student are able to articulate clear goals and the means by which they can be achieved. The faculty representative can be helpful in this process by sharing with the field instructor the structures used in facilitating classroom work which have been successful in responding to the needs of the handicapped student.[7]

The issue of confidentiality may arise when a handicapped student requires an attendant, or an interpreter to be present during contacts with clients. The field instructor and student need to prepare clients for the presence of another person and need to inform the attendant or interpreter about the importance of confidentiality.

It has been observed that for some clients the fact of a handicapped worker creates a conflict in that they may feel reluctant to share problems with someone whose life situation seems so much worse than their own. Field instructors can be helpful in encouraging students to address this issue with clients.[8]

A dilemma in placing the handicapped student is the question of whether to use a rehabilitation setting. Some students and practicum co-ordinators are strongly opposed to such placements which are seen as a strong statement that handicapped students have only limited options and must be restricted to work with other handicapped persons. While this may be an accurate assumption of prejudice if the selection is made without thought and solely in response to the handicap factor, placement in a rehabilitation setting should not be rejected with a similar reflex reaction. In a rehabilitation setting, acceptance and understanding can be mutual and can work in the service of both the student and the clients and their families. Students in both rehabilitation settings and other settings must learn to work with non-handicapped staff, families of their clients, and other non-handicapped people in the community resource system. Another important factor is the availability of employment opportunities for the handicapped person, a factor that varies from community to community but which must be considered when selecting a practicum site. Sensitivity, humour, and openness in communication are of particular importance in helping both field instructor, student, and other staff to make the practicum a successful one. Modelling of openness, sensitivity, and humour on the part of the field instructor will help the student to relate to clients and co-workers in a similar manner. The goal for all parties is to recognize the handicap but not to let it take over or dominate the relationship between student and client, field instructor, or others.

Notes

1 Suanna J. Wilson, *Field Instruction: Techniques for Supervision* (New York: Macmillan, 1981), p. 195.

2 Veronica Coulshed, Ric Woods and Herb Wiseman, "Failing to Fail Students: Views of Fieldwork Supervisors," 1985, Faculty of Social Work, Wilfrid Laurier University, p. 4

3 Some of the ideas presented here are based on Wilson, *Field Instruction,* pp. 198-203.

4 Judith Mishne, "Narcissistic Vulnerability of the Younger Student: The Need for Non-Confrontive Empathic Supervision," *The Clinical Supervisor* 1 (Summer 1983): 3-12.

5 Alfred Kadushin, "Games People Play in Supervision," *Social Work* 13 (July 1968): 23-32; Lillian Hawthorne, "Games Supervisors Play," *Social Work* 20 (May 1975): 179-183.

6 Kadushin, "Games People Play in Supervision," p. 27.

7 Lauren Krinsky Weinberg, "Unique Learning Needs of Physically Handicapped Social Work Students," *Journal of Education for Social Work* 14 (Winter 1978): 110.

8 Ibid., p. 115.

9

Ethnically-Sensitive Field Instruction: A Necessity in a Multicultural Society*

By Esther Blum†

The multicultural reality in Canada can no longer be ignored. The 1981 census shows that one third of the population has roots which are other than English or French. Sixteen percent of the population are immigrants or refugees and the indigenous people comprise more than two percent. Larger numbers of people than ever before are coming from non-Western societies. The implications for social workers are many. Increasingly we must provide services for people who are unfamiliar with or distrust professional helping. Research has demonstrated that mainstream social services are often inaccessible to minority ethnic people (that is, non-English or French in origin) due to cultural, linguistic or organizational barriers.[1] One step to overcoming these obstacles is recruiting and training students from different ethnic groups to become social workers. These ethnic minority social workers can then not only assist their own communities but as well educate others who provide social services.

Students from ethnic minority backgrounds (especially recent immigrants and refugees, Natives and foreign students) often bring issues and knowledge to field instruction which are very different from those of the mainstream student. It is very easy for their prime anxieties and difficulties to be overlooked in the attempt to focus on areas of learning which are similar to all students. By so doing the field instruction is, albeit inadvertently, giving minority students the message that their issues are not important and that to be successful students and social workers they must comply with the majority. This is an assimilationist

---

*This chapter discusses ethno-sensitive issues in field instruction within the Canadian multi-cultural context. The authors believe that the concepts are transferable and can be used in other countries.

†Esther Blum, M.S.W. is Assistant Professor, University of Manitoba, School of Social Work and a Doctoral Candidate, University of Toronto, Faculty of Social Work.

position which belies both the multicultural reality of our population and the multicultural policies of our Government. The social workers we graduate will not be prepared to work with different ethnic communities. Ethnically sensitive field instructors by encouraging minority students to air their concerns and ideas can provide better education for all students as well as for themselves. They also can assist in laying the groundwork for better services to ethnic minority people.

POTENTIAL AREAS OF CULTURAL CLASH

Misunderstandings between field instructors and students occur frequently for many reasons, not the least of which are different cultural expectations and attitudes. Three areas affected by the culture of origin and consequent worldviews are: a) the expectations of the instructor-student relationship, b) the attitudes toward agency "authority", c) the student's understanding of the helping process. Potential clashes in these areas will be briefly elaborated below.

Seeking help in some cultures is a very private matter. Families and close friends are the most usual helpers. Confidences are shared with clergymen, doctors and other healers only when the primary helpers are absent or unable to assist. For many students teachers are to be listened to, but rarely questioned and never challenged. For students to share personal and academic difficulties is to lower their esteem and evaluation in the eyes of the teacher. Yet, in field instruction we expect students as learners to be aware of and discuss both their strengths and weaknesses. A part of the learning process entails examining mistakes and searching for future alternatives. When students are unable to participate in this process, it is important to explore the possibility that their resistance has cultural underpinnings. They may have no models for the expected instructor-student behaviour; in fact their previous educational experiences may completely contradict such behaviour. Reaching out for help or disagreeing with the instructor's views may be similarly foreign activities. Since changing these behaviours requires challenging deeply ingrained values such as respect for elders and educated people it is often insufficient to understand the new set of expectations alone. As field instructors we need to give these students support and encouragement. However, we must also be aware of our power as socialization agents. Are our ways of teaching and learning the best ones? Do we have the right to impose them on others?

Very much related to the issues discussed above are those arising from differing views of the student role and agency authority. How much initiative should a student take? Should they challenge colleagues or supervisors? Let me illustrate with a case example from my own experience as field instructor.

Peter was a very capable final year B.S.W. student from Hong Kong. He was assigned several clients and also asked to run a group of isolated refugee women. He tackled all of these activities enthusiastically and creatively. Yet at every field meeting he arrived in "crisis." These "crises" (to use his own words) were not those typical of other students who might be organizing their first group or entering a difficult stage in the helping process. They were "crises" over meeting with other workers to discuss intervention strategies for clients common to them both, or "crises" over requesting additional space or funds for the group, or over conflicting commitments when the agency director called a staff conference. I found myself getting impatient with what I initially assessed to be exaggerated reactions to very common and easily handled situations. However, upon further reflection I realized that there was a common thread to all of these "crises". Each situation required that he question the decisions of either the agency director or other professional staff. It meant he was challenging the hierarchical structure that he had been taught was the good and natural order of things; it was inviolable. The internal conflicts set up by the opposing professional and cultural dictates were indeed causing a crisis in his life.

Recognizing the magnitude of the crisis, exploring the dynamics of the conflict and changing my attitude toward the problem were the key ingredients to helping the student deal with these situations. It is essential that we realize that people from other backgrounds may have different experiences and beliefs about authority relationships, about education and about helping.

Student ideas about the nature of the helping process are sometimes in conflict with notions of professional helping. For people from some cultures, professional helping is an unknown entity; other people may approve of practical help from "strangers" but allow only family and close friends to administer to social and emotional wounds; still others may accept social workers only after a long trust building period; others look to social workers as wise people and experts. When students are working with members of their own ethnic group, they may well understand the cultural imperatives of helping better than their field instructors. This can be threatening to the instructors who not only perceive themselves to be without a role and function but also who discover their helping interventions inappropriate and ineffective. The most difficult task may be accepting the validity of other helping approaches. Instructors may spend more time as "learners" of the culture and ways of the community, however their role as teacher remains. They must encourage the student to analyze and adapt existing helping theories or to create new ones. Exploring together ways of accessing mainstream services or advocating for and developing programs appropriate for minorities might occupy more of the field instruction time. As well, many minority students need support and skills to cope with the unconscious and conscious messages of discrimination they encounter daily in the social and service systems. Of any students, they are the most likely to "burnout" before they even enter the employment force because they are bombarded by inequity constantly—at home, at work, in school and in society. Their educational program must provide some basic tools to help them confront and educate other service providers.

While dealing with the issues of discrimination in the mainstream system, students are agonizing too over how they will be accepted by their own communities now that they are becoming "professionals". Are they "selling out" to mainstream values? The sensitive field instructor can help students sort out their emerging professional identity and their ethnic identity.

When ethnic minority students are working with mainstream clients and programs, the field instructors' roles are somewhat different. They become the major socializing agents and cultural informants. This is easily accomplished when the issue is simply a lack of information about the service system. However, when the student's meaning of help clashes with the professional (and mainstream) view of help, the task is more difficult, and sometimes painful. It often calls into question students' fundamental assumptions about human beings and interaction. The students' self esteem and self image may be sorely shaken during this process. Field instructors need to be sensitive to this internal upheaval and as in the previous situation to assist students as they struggle towards a new definition of their ethnicity as well as a professional identity.

A brief word about the dual identity crisis of ethnic minority students and the dual socialization role of field instructors. All students of social work deal with issues around their developing professional identity. All field instructors help socialize students to the social work profession. With increased information about mainstream culture through professional socialization ethnic minority students also must cope with a potentially changing ethnic or cultural identification. So that personal conflicts can be minimized and their strengths emphasized consideration should be given to the type of agency placement these students are assigned. It would seem that an organization compatible either structurally or culturally with students' worldviews would facilitate the field instruction process and enhance the learning experience immensely. Field instructors could concentrate on their role as professional socialization agents primarily. Students could deal with acquiring one new identity at a time.

THE ETHNICITY OF THE FIELD INSTRUCTOR

Concluding my comments without mentioning the variable of field instructor ethnicity in the student-instructor interaction might leave the reader with the assumption that all field instructors are from the ethnic majority cultures. This is clearly not the case. Although the largest number of ethnic minority students will probably be paired with field instructors of either English or French heritages, other combinations will include ethnic minority students with field instructors from the same ethnic background and ethnic minority students with field instructors from different ethnic minority communities. In addition to the general areas of concern outlined in the previous section, each of these configurations carries particular issues.

a) Majority Group Field Instructor – Minority Group Student

There is a tendency in Canadian society to ignore cultural and racial differences in order to uphold the tenets of equality. It is thought that treating people equally means treating everyone as if they were similar. The experiences of ethnic minorities are often similar neither socially, economically nor culturally. Ignoring these differences sets the stage for misconceptions, faulty communication and potentially negative learning experiences. Students try to be people they cannot be, and instructors miss out on the opportunity to enhance their understanding of the wider multicultural society. Openly exploring differences between cultural assumptions and expectations not only validates what might be important parts of students' lives but also encourages them to ask questions and examine the norms of the majority society in a non-threatening environment for perhaps the first time. As mentioned previously, field instructors thus serve both as professional and societal socialization agents. Since the impact may extend well beyond students' professional lives, it is doubly critical that majority group field instructors be aware of the messages they are giving to ethnic minority students. It is also important that these field instructors be prepared to spend more time learning about the cultures of their ethnic minority students.

b) Field Instructor and Student – Same Ethnic Minorities

Rather than socialization agents, minority field instructors may serve as models and cultural mediators for students of the same ethnic background. Students may feel more comfortable sharing issues of concern stemming from value and worldview conflicts. Alternatively, field instructors may pick up on these concerns more quickly because of their common heritage. Field instructors, however, must guard against feelings of over-identification with students. When this occurs students are often treated too leniently and not pushed to achieve their potential, or the expectations placed upon them are far beyond those of other students. Either way student education suffers. An advantage that minority group field instructors working with students from their own background have over majority group instructors is that they have more tools to differentiate normal and deviant student behaviour. Minority students have commented that they cannot hide behind excuses of linguistic inability or cultural misunderstanding when their field instructor is "one of their own." The majority field instructor while being open and tolerant to difference must guard against culture becoming an excuse for incompetence.

c) Field Instructor and Student – Different Ethnic Minorities
Again in the instance of the field instructor and student from two different minority groups the airing of differences and inter-group perceptions is critical to both a good beginning and continuing relationship. Constant checking of assumptions will ensure misunderstandings are quickly resolved. Depending on the field instructors' facility in mainstream society, they may either become socialization agents or cultural interpreters. Because of the shared status of "ethnic minority" a bond of understanding may be formed more quickly than with instructors from the majority group. Instructors may become models for the students. They too, however, must be wary of over-identification with the students' struggles. Unlike their counterparts in the last section, they can well be fooled into sanctioning less than competent work since they are less knowledgeable of the students' cultural environment.

A fourth combination we will not elaborate on here since the focus is ethnic minority students, is the minority field instructor and the ethnic majority student. Suffice it to say that the issues albeit somewhat different are similar in that for two or more people of different ethnic backgrounds to work together successfully the cultural dimension of learning and practice must be addressed. This latter point is key to all ethnically-sensitive field instruction.

Cultural pluralism is the philosophy guiding this discussion. I do not believe that we can help students grow without offering them choices. We cannot offer them choices without being as clear about their realities as they must be about ours. We must also be prepared to accept that their alternatives may be better than ours. They must be prepared to pay the price that mainstream society exacts for being different. Unfortunately, we still live in an assimilationist society. Fortunately, the tides may be changing.

Notes

1 Anna Bodnar and M. Reimer, *The Organization of Social Services and its Implications for the Mental Health of Immigrant Women* (Ottawa: Secretary of State, [1979]); Canadian Mental Health Association, Manitoba Division, *A Report on Mental Health Needs of Southeast Asian Refugees* (Winnipeg: The Refugee Mental Health Planning Committee, [1982]); M. Nair, "New Immigrants Use of Four Social Service Agencies in a Canadian Metropolis" (D.S.W. dissertation, Columbia University, 1978).

10 Legal Aspects of Field Instruction

This chapter is cautionary. It deals with some of the legal issues which may arise when a student who is not an employee of the agency enters into a working/learning relationship with the agency, the field instructor, and clients served by that agency. Legislation differs and the extent of insurance coverage will vary among universities, agencies, and professional bodies. This discussion, therefore, will deal with legal issues in general. It is advisable for agency directors to clarify questions of legal liability with the practicum co-ordinator. It may be necessary to consult with the respective insurance carriers that serve both the university and the agency in order to clarify the precise nature of the coverage provided in situations of off-campus education. The legal accountability of social workers and social work students to their clients and of field instructors to social work students is an open question. Social workers, regardless of their level of training, present themselves to the public as possessing particular knowledge and skills whether there is a direct contractual relationship as a result of a fee for service or whether that service is provided by child welfare agencies, correctional systems, or mental health and educational facilities.[1]

DISCLOSURE OF STUDENT STATUS

The issue of disclosure to clients regarding the student's status as a student and the consequent limitation on their time with the agency is one that has been perceived as equivocal. Social work educators have avoided taking a position preferring to leave the decision to the agency which may or may not have developed a policy. It is an issue, however, that has both legal and ethical consequences.

To claim professional status is to acknowledge rights and responsibilities of the parties to the professional relationship. To become a professional takes training and the public should be as aware of the existence of a supervised practice training requirement for social work as it is of the need for a similar phase of medical or legal education.[2]

There has been a momentum recently, created by the consumer rights movement, that is exerting pressure on all professionals toward full disclosure to patients or clients of matters that affect their treatment or involvement with a specific service. There is no doubt that a full disclosure would include the qualifications and status of the professional staff. In general, there is less question about the identification of social work student status for those doing a hospital-based practicum. Other settings, however, may not be so clear about this issue.

Some of the arguments against disclosure are rooted in the fear of losing clients or jeoparizing the formation of a working relationship either because of lack of belief in a student's professional expertise or reluctance to engage in a relationship where termination is inevitable when the practicum ends. These do not seem to be compelling arguments when weighed against the value of encouraging the student to establish an honest basis for a working relationship. The terms of the disclosure include the fact that a skilled field instructor is the third party in the working relationship.

Field instructors should discuss this issue with their students and review with them the process of informing clients about the student social worker, field instructor, and client relationship. Students' fears and feelings about their student status can then be discussed and client reactions anticipated. Students need to be reminded and reassured that they do bring some knowledge and expertise to the practicum. Student status does not denote incompetence but rather the need for the student to acquire additional experience and knowledge by working closely with an experienced worker within that agency. If students and field instructors view disclosure of student status as demeaning, then this attitude will, of course, be transmitted to the client.

PRIVILEGED COMMUNICATIONS AND CONFIDENTIALITY

It is important for field instructors and students to be aware of issues regarding confidentiality and privileged communications because social workers are being asked to testify on such matters as adoptions, child custody and welfare matters, or a client's mental state. In addition, they may be compelled by the court to reveal information they have gained during individual or group counselling sessions.[3] No privilege attaches to communications made by a client to a social worker. Canadian law extends privilege only to communications made to a lawyer by his client. Legislation differs among the fifty states; a protected communication or relationship that may be kept out of legal proceedings in one state may not be regarded as privileged in another state. Accordingly, the social worker/client relationship varies from state to state as the legislatures and judiciary weigh the merits of disclosure to arrive at the truth opposed to the need to protect a relationship built on trust and confidentiality.

If social workers are subpoened to testify in court, they cannot be held liable for what they say in court by the client. They may be held responsible to their clients, however, for failing to inform clients of the possibility that they may be compelled to testify concerning the nature and content of the work with the client.[4] It is also important to be aware that records and notes made by a social worker may be subpoened and entered in evidence if such material is deemed relevant by the judge.

Field instructors should inform students that they must let clients know in advance of interviews if the possibility exists that they may be required to testify in regard to that client's situation. It is also important that records and notes be kept up to date as the situation develops and that they be objective and based on observed facts. Students should be informed that they are not compelled to give any information by telephone to anyone, including lawyers. Requests for information must be in writing and any responses should be thoroughly discussed with students.

Students are naturally fearful that disclosure to clients, that what transpires in an interview may not be held in confidence, may jeopardize the trusting relationship they wish to establish. The conflict arises where social work intervention is both statutory and preventive or therapeutic. A difficult area for field instruction is the reconciliation of the use of authority with social work values. In many settings, the student must establish a relationship with a client that is prefaced by the knowledge that information regarding violent behaviour or child abuse may not be held in confidence between client and social worker. Students must be informed that in most jurisdictions, child welfare laws compel people working in professional capacities to report suspicions of child abuse to the local child welfare authority.

Some states in the United States and some Canadian jurisdictions have enacted special statutes wherein a judge can grant privileged communication to a professional, usually a psychiatrist or a psychologist. It is instructive to review the classic conceptual test, developed by Wigmore, which is used by courts both in the United States and Canada as a standard in deciding whether a communication is privileged. The relevant standards are:

1. The communication must originate in the confidence that it will not be disclosed.
2. The element of confidentiality must be essential to the full and satisfactory maintenance of the relationship between the parties.
3. The relationship must be one that in the opinion of the community ought to be fostered.
4. The injury to the relationship that would ensue through a disclosure of the communications must be greater than the benefit gained from the outcome of the litigation if it should succeed.[5]

INFORMED CONSENT

Field instructors should be certain that students understand the meaning and importance of informed consent. Technology has produced computer-stored information banks, audio and video taping, and interviews conducted before a one-way vision mirror behind which are persons unknown to the clients. Consumer protection activity has increased sensitivity to clients' vulnerability to the omission of informed consent procedures or even to hastily and perfunctorily presented explanations. Field instructors should discuss with students the fact that clients' anxiety about problems may interfere with the ability to understand what is being asked or explained. Consent, to be informed, must be made truly and simply comprehensible to clients. Many agencies have policies regarding informed consent procedures and in some jurisdictions, patients and clients may have legal recourse if their right to be informed and to give proper consent has been violated.

MALPRACTICE LIABILITY

Malpractice is a specialized form of negligence that must contain these elements to establish a legal basis for action. The elements are summarized as follows:
1. A duty, or obligation, recognized by the law, requiring the actor to conform to a certain standard of conduct.
2. A failure on his part to conform to the standards required.
3. A reasonably close causal connection between the conduct and the resulting injury.
4. Actual loss or damage resulting to the interests (health, finances, and emotional or psychological ability) of another.[6]

Though malpractice litigation and liability has captured public attention because of the escalating cost of liability insurance, malpractice charges made against social work practitioners are still relatively uncommon events. In a recent study in New Jersey, one hundred and five social workers responded to a questionnaire survey that was designed to elicit the respondent's awareness of existing malpractice litigation, the steps social workers would take to protect themselves, and knowledge about conditions that could lead to successful malpractice litigation. The survey revealed that bases for reported litigation against social workers include a client's suicide, a bungled child abuse case, and a breach of confidentiality, but none of the plaintifs won their case in court.[7] These findings notwithstanding, at least two agencies in New Jersey where field instruction is provided to social work students, require that students carry their own malpractice insurance.[8]

In Canada, there was one civil complaint lodged against a social worker that did not succeed and a situation in which three Children's

Aid Society workers were charged under the *Criminal Code* of exposing a child under 10 years of age to dangers to its life or health. This case too, did not succeed in Court.[9]

In 1979, all of the accredited graduate schools of social work in the United States were asked by the Council on Social Work Education whether malpractice insurance for students was required. Their report stated that most schools (73%) did not have a policy on the issue of malpractice insurance for students. This lack of policy and concern with the issue also was indicated by the fact that only 19% of the responding schools provided premiums for the students.[10] The authors' conclusion is that though there is little case law involving malpractice suits brought against social work psychotherapists, one could make a case for insurance coverage for students placed in settings where psychotherapy is the dominant mode of intervention, to be paid for either by the school, the agency, or the student.[11]

STRATEGY FOR COLLECTIVE AGREEMENT STRIKES

A situation of great concern to social work educators, both within the university and the agency, is the effect on students completing a practicum, when strikes of organized workers occur. Many agency employees, both professional workers and support staff, belong to bargaining units. When collective agreement negotiations break down, various degrees of action or slow down may occur, a strike may be called, pickets may ring the agency, and the student may be caught in the conflict. Feelings run high and students may become politicized and identified with either side of the conflict as well as with clients whose welfare may be in jeopardy because of the disruption. In addition, for a student, the practicum is endangered because of lost time, or a striking field instructor. If the disruption occurs near the beginning of the practicum, the school may help the student negotiate an alternate placement. However, where half or more of the practicum has been completed, the faculty representative and the field instructor will have to help the student make a decision about what action to take. Under no circumstances should students be required to cross a picket line, or be used as substitutes for striking workers.

SEXUAL HARASSMENT

Sexual harassment has come into public consciousness in the last decade and most universities have developed policies and procedural mechanisms to deal with complaints when they occur in the classroom or on campus. In general, students have sought protection from and redress against unwanted sexual overtures from faculty who take advantage of an unequal power balance between professor and student.

This issue becomes more complicated when it moves away from the campus and into a social agency. There is usually no explicit agency policy in regard to sexual harassment and the student may feel more vulnerable to any behaviour which seems to make a sexual demand, whether real or imagined. Schools must develop policy through student-faculty discussion so that students will feel able to consult the faculty if a situation arises that they feel unable to control. Field instructor-student relationship is similar to worker-client relationship and demands the same ethical injunctions of respect and concern for dignity and individual rights. Attraction may be mutual, but both field instructor and student are well advised to complete the practicum relationship before embarking on a more intimate one.

Notes

1 Elaine Vayda and Mary Satterfield, *Law for Social Workers: A Canadian Guide* (Toronto: Carswell, 1984), p. 269.
2 Harriet R. Feiner and Elsbeth Couch, "I've Got a Secret: The Student in the Agency," *Social Casework* 66 (May 1985): 274.
3 Barton Bernstein, "Privileged Communications to the Social Worker," *Social Work* 22 (July 1977): 264-268.
4 Ibid., p. 266.
5 John H. Wigmore. *Evidence*, Vol. 8 (3rd Ed.) McNaughton Rev. (New York: Little, Brown & Co., 1961), p. 528. Quoted in Ibid., p. 265.
6 Wilson Prosser. *Handbook of the Law of Torts* (4th Ed.), (St. Paul, Minn: West Publishing Co., 1971). Quoted in Ronald K. Green and Gibbi Cox, "Social Work and Malpractice: A Converging Course," *Social Work* 29 (March 1984): 100.
7 Ursula Gerhard and Alexander D. Brooks, "Social Workers and Malpractice: Law, Attitudes, and Knowledge," *Social Casework* 66 (September 1985): 413.
8 Ibid., p. 411.
9 Unreported civil charge mentioned in OAPSW Newsmagazine, November 1985 and charges under Criminal Code case reported in OAPSW Newsmagazine, Fall 1982.
10 Donald C. Dendinger, Roger Hille, and Iona T. Bulkins, "Malpractice Insurance for Practicum Students—An Emergency Need?" *Journal of Education for Social Work* 18 (Winter 1982): 75.
11 Ibid., p. 78.

11 Evaluation

The only valid assessment of learning especially in professional education, is performance in the carrying out of the professional role under either real or simulated conditions.[1]

Evaluation is the determination of the extent to which a student has achieved the objectives of a particular learning activity. Evaluation of learning in field practice describes the student's current level of knowledge and skill, may identify the progress and difficulties experienced in arriving at that point, and specifies areas for future development.[2] Ongoing, or formative, evaluations that provide continuous specific feedback keep the focus on incremental learning. Through numerous evaluations the field instructor helps the student move through retrieval of practice behaviours, reflection about those events, linkage to social work knowledge, and the formulation of new professional responses.

STRESS FACTORS

Evaluation produces stress for both student and instructor. In a study of field instructors, Gitterman and Gitterman found 87% of those surveyed experienced stress in evaluation related to defining criteria, writing the formal document, assessing student practice, and engaging the student in the evaluation process.[3] Kadushin's study of social work supervisors found that supervisors disliked evaluation as it reminded them of the status differential between themselves and their workers and highlighted the power inherent in their role.[4] Supervisors perceived the evaluation of the worker's performance as an indirect evaluation of the supervisor's effectiveness and helpfulness. There was also concern that a negative evaluation would evoke anger and would upset the balance that had been established in the worker/supervisor relationship. Field instructors may experience student evaluation as a reflection of their teaching competence. Instructors question whether they chose enough appropriate assignments for student learning to take place, whether they spent enough time with the student, whether they provided enough support, or challenge. Instructors wonder whether students have heard the critical feedback provided throughout the term so that the final evaluation will not come as a surprise. Instructors may be apprehensive about the student's feedback regarding their teaching, especially if the student has not been forthcoming throughout the term. Instructors question their own standards in regard to expectations, and most struggle with the scarcity of objective criteria that can be used to evaluate social work student performance. When instructors must give negative feedback they have concerns about whether the school will support them if the student launches a grievance or appeal.

Students experience anxiety and insecurity as a normal and inevitable part of evaluation. Ongoing positive and negative feedback throughout the term will diminish apprehension about the final evaluation. Nevertheless, students tend to feel vulnerable regarding the instructor's power in evaluation and grading. Student reaction to identification of their strengths and weaknesses is unique based on their comfort level with receiving critical feedback and their expectations of themselves as learners and performers. For example, students accustomed to positive feedback may react to the identification of problem areas with disappointment or anger. However, students who have found it difficult to learn social work skills may be pleased with the balance of strengths and weaknesses described in the evaluation.

EVALUATION AS ONGOING FEEDBACK

Since both instructor and student experience evaluation as stressful, it is critical that ongoing discussion about the process and outcome of the field practicum be a feature of field learning. Specifically, contracting can be seen as a continuous mutual process which includes clarification of objectives and outcomes of learning, feedback to the student regarding progress in meeting those objectives, and feedback to the instructor regarding the effectiveness of the field instruction. One obstacle to achieving this degree of openness is the student's feelings of vulnerability in relation to the power of the instructor. Students are often reluctant and fearful to express concerns or to give instructors feedback about the effect of their teaching. Therefore, instructors have to help students learn how to give feedback to those in authority. In Chapter 2 we discussed the ecological perspective in social work noting the necessity for students to learn how to influence organizational decisions in the interests of enhanced service delivery. Influence includes the ability to present critical feedback effectively, most often to those who have power. Learning to give and use feedback in the field instructor/student relationship can prepare the student to be an effective professional worker in an organization. Instructors must take initiative and responsibility to help students learn these behaviours by reaching for feedback, demonstrating to students that their input will be heard and discussed. This reinforces the learning/teaching enterprise as a mutual endeavour.

Wilson points out that through continuous sharing of impressions, critiques, and suggestions for improvement, the student becomes aware of areas where growth is needed and can use the suggested techniques to develop new practice skill.[5] If practice experience is not continuously evaluated, both field instructors and students may miss the opportunity for reflection, linkage, and understanding of practice competence. Sharing evaluative feedback only at the end deprives the student of the opportunity to work on weak areas and move towards meeting objectives.

It is useful to structure formal review periods to examine the student's progress and practice in relation to the objectives. Reviews provide the opportunity to clarify issues, develop more focus for the next stage of learning, and enable students to act on the feedback and incorporate it in current practice. Though final evaluations should contain no surprises, Pennell has pointed out that the process of a broadened final examination of the student's work may reveal new perceptions of the student's approach to practice.[6] Patterns may appear which are not good practice. Students must be made aware of these patterns so that they can consciously attempt to modify their behaviour in their future work. It is questionable whether field instructors should include these perceptions in the final evaluation because they have appeared only at the end of the practicum. Field instructors may wish to consult the faculty representative about this issue.

OBJECTIVE CRITERIA

Evaluation must be based on clear criteria which are used by the student and field instructor as the framework for the practicum. Schools of social work define objectives for practicum learning that reflect knowledge, value, and skill expectations to be achieved. Evaluation is aided by objectives that are clear, specific, and expressed in behavioural terms defining what it is that a student is expected to do in order to meet a particular objective. As discussed in Chapter 6 general objectives of the school's practicum provide a framework. These objectives are useful insofar as they can be concretized and reflect the activities of the particular practice of that field setting. Discussing these objectives with the student at the beginning of the practicum provides an opportunity to clarify concepts and meanings. Through this process students become familiar with what they are required to learn and can participate more actively in their own learning. By referring to objectives throughout the field instruction process, students are enabled to make changes in their professional practice. Objectives also provide a conceptual framework for students to link practice behaviours to a social work knowledge base.

At the beginning of the practicum students vary in their skill and knowledge level. Therefore, it is likely that they will vary in the extent to which they achieve objectives at the end. The importance of change and individual development are central values in social work practice and influence field instruction. If students who began with little or no experience, knowledge, and skill begin to make positive changes, instructors value that gain. However, development alone is not sufficient. A student must reach a minimum level of competence in order to achieve a passing grade. This often presents a dilemma for a field instructor where a student has not quite met expectations. As movement has been demonstrated there is a desire to reward that gain. Field instructors may hope that if the student moves into a continuing phase of the educational process (second-level practicum, employment, or advanced degree program) further growth will occur and a satisfactory performance level will emerge. Passing the student ahead, based on this hope, may leave the student struggling in each successive experience to "catch up" to ever increasing expectations. Instructors may find they need to recommend extensions or repeats of the practicum so that the student who has begun to develop necessary knowledge and skill is given additional time to meet the standards of the current level of education.

LINKAGE TO THE LEARNING CONTRACT

As discussed in Chapter 6, contracting involves setting individualized objectives for a particular student. A baseline assessment of the student's level of knowledge and skill was formulated at the beginning of the practicum. By comparing this assessment to the practicum objectives, a determination of what needs to be learned is made. Learning activities, resources, and techniques can be chosen or designed so that the learning objectives can be achieved. The method of evaluation is also contracted at the beginning, including which persons other than the field instructor will be consulted and what concrete evidence will be used, such as tapes or reports.

MAINTAINING OBJECTIVITY

The position of the field instructor as teacher and socializing agent, and the intensity of teaching in a dyad may compromise the instructor's objectivity in evaluation. Recognizing this, Wilson provides some useful suggestions.[7] She advises a period of reflection as the first step in preparing for the evaluation. Instructors consider their own feelings about appraisals in general, about writing this evaluation, about committing their thoughts regarding the student to paper. She suggests reviewing the experience with the student, recalling the beginning, highlights along the way, what is important for the next instructor or employer to know about the student, and feelings the instructor has about the student that have never been shared. In this way positive or negative biases that may act as obstacles to objectivity are identified.

While reviewing the student's practice it is important to differentiate between knowledge and skill and the student's personality. Assessments of the student's personality are not an appropriate part of educational evaluations. However, when the student's personality interferes with practice performance this should be addressed by using a practice example to demonstrate the interference. For example, it is not appropriate to label a student as aggressive and hostile. Rather, persistent inability to establish co-operative relationships with colleagues, angry outbursts, or attacking other's intentions, are concrete demonstrations of a personality difficulty.

Objectivity is enhanced by specificity of objectives. Brennan notes that the more general the guideline for evaluation, the more opportunity for subjectivity.[8] Time spent in contracting and re-contracting so that outcome behaviours are clearly understood facilitates student learning and final evaluation.

Objectivity is enhanced by using accurate information to form a judgment. In Chapter 7 we discussed the strengths and weaknesses in using methods that provide direct access to practice data, and methods that involve indirect access. Actual data is likely to be more accurate than reports in assessing knowledge and skill of interactional processes. Reports are useful in evaluating conceptual and written skills.

It is not unusual for student performance to be inconsistent based on the nature of the practice task as well as idiosyncratic factors. Multiple observations of the student's work provide a more adequate data base on which to make accurate judgments.[9]

Multiple reviewers can also add to objectivity in evaluation. Some instructors contract for other social workers in the agency to participate in aspects of the evaluation. In some schools, faculty members or other field instructors, will also review samples of the student's practice.

Kadushin describes some classic pitfalls supervisors experience in evaluating workers.

These include the 'error of central tendency' – the tendency, when in doubt, to rate specific aspects of the worker's performance as 'fair' or 'average'; the 'halo effect' – the tendency to make a global judgment about the worker's performance and then to perceive all aspects of the worker's performance as consistent with that general judgment; the 'contrast error' – the tendency to evaluate using onself as a standard, the very conscientious supervisor seeing most workers as less conscientious, the highly organized supervisor tending to see others as less well organized; 'leniency bias'–a reluctance to evaluate negatively and critically.[10]

PREPARATION FOR THE EVALUATION CONFERENCE

In preparing for the conference both student and instructor should clarify all aspects of format in advance such as length of the conference and advance preparation. The contract should be reviewed, and the agreements made regarding evaluation used. Objectives and forms provided by the school for evaluation should be available in advance of the conference. If a rating scale is to be used, the definitions and guidelines for rating should be clear and understood by student and instructor. Data on which to base judgments should be accessible to both participants. If other personnel are to be involved in evaluation both student and instructor should choose a sample of materials to be reviewed.

The student and instructor should discuss the procedures they will follow so that each is clear about expectations and responsibilities. It is useful for the instructor to review the objectives and the practice material and make rough notes highlighting conclusions so that the conference can be used for discussion.

THE EVALUATION CONFERENCE

As the student is likely to be anxious about the final evaluation, Kadushin suggests opening the conference by presenting a general evaluation of performance in simple, clear, and unambiguous terms.[11] Discussion is then held regarding the achievement of objectives and specific practice illustrations are used by the field instructor and student to support the judgments. Gitterman and Gitterman suggest the field instructor focus the discussion emphasizing the details of the student's practice and learning.[12] Themes will be identified, areas of mastery highlighted, as well as problem areas, and areas for further growth. The field instructor offers explicit feedback and helps the student to actively participate, to offer self-appraisal, and to raise disagreements with the instructor's perceptions and assessment. The context of learning, that is, the organizational characteristics and the nature of the practice assignments should also be examined in relation to facilitating or constraining the student's learning.

Instructors are sensitive to the student's reactions and attempt to openly discuss issues and concerns. If the student and instructor have been able to develop effective communication throughout the learning process they will be able to deal with negative and positive reactions regarding evaluation. If the student and instructor have experienced difficulty with open and direct feedback, with management of disagreements and conflict, then these problems are likely to appear again in the evaluation conference.

Discussion of the dynamics of teaching and learning as they relate to the particular student and instructor are an important part of evaluation. The student's learning style and pace, the instructor's educational approaches, and the interactions between the two are subject to evaluation. Students should be encouraged to evaluate the educational effectiveness of the field setting, the assignments carried, the activities attended, and the process of field instruction itself. As most students are fearful that a critical evaluation will negatively effect their grade, it is advisable that the evaluation of the student's performance be submitted to the school before students are asked to evaluate their practicum. It is disheartening for instructors to learn, after the fact, what the student was thinking, feeling, and experiencing and not have had the opportunity to attempt to change their interaction. Throughout this book, we have encouraged field instructors to elicit ongoing feedback and demonstrate to the student that it is safe to be critical.

Among the Canadian schools participating in the Field Instructor Training Project twelve schools have formal procedures to evaluate field instructors and five schools do not. Of the twelve schools who have procedures, five are compulsory and seven are voluntary. It is essential for students and instructors to be familiar with the guidelines and criteria for this evaluation at the outset of the practicum. As we have indicated, formal evaluation is usually done after the student's evaluation and grades have been submitted. We recommend that field instructors have a copy of any written evaluation of their work.

THE WRITTEN EVALUATION

Each school of social work has procedures for writing and submitting the final evaluation. In most schools the field instructor takes responsibility for writing the final evaluation following the school's guidelines. If rating scales are used, definitions should be clear and understood. Field instructors generally recommend a grade and the faculty representative gives the grade based on the written evaluation. In some schools the practicum is a credit/no credit course, in others there are numerical or letter grades.

Wilson gives many guidelines for the written document.[13] It should be clear, factual, and specific. Descriptions and significant comments should be substantiated with brief practice examples. It should clearly label areas of mastery, problem areas, and areas for further growth. If a rating scale is used there should be congruence between the narrative section and the final rating.

The written evaluation should be prepared as soon after the evaluation conference as possible. The student should have the opportunity to express any feelings about the written evaluation or to request changes in specific parts. If the instructor does not agree some schools suggest that the student attach their own written statement to the evaluation. If there is a question, the faculty representative should be consulted for specific assistance and clarification of procedures. Schools have grievance and appeal mechanisms which the student may want to use to settle a major disagreement regarding evaluation. The student should read the evaluation and sign it indicating that it has been read. If the student reads the evaluation and refuses to sign it, this should be documented.

The original written evaluation is the property of the school and is placed on the student's record. In most schools, the student and instructor keep a copy. The evaluation is not subject to disclosure without the student's consent. Schools have policies regarding use of the evaluation for reference purposes. It is useful to be familiar with these policies.

APPEALS

Most schools have formal grievance or appeal procedures for students to challenge academic decisions including practicum grades. Before reaching the appeal stage efforts are generally made to resolve disagreements through regular procedures, such as review meetings with the faculty representative and the practicum co-ordinator. If these methods are unsuccessful the student may, during a specific time period, present a written request for an appeal hearing. A designated person or committee, usually the chairperson or members of the appeal committee decides whether there are sufficient grounds to hold a formal appeal. The appeal committee usually consists of faculty members and students. As field related issues are often heard before the appeal committee it is of concern and importance that field instructors also comprise part of the membership of an appeal committee.

In preparation for the appeal the student gathers support for their case, may contact witnesses to appear at the hearing, and may bring an advocate such as another student, a faculty member, or a lawyer. The field instructor and faculty representative should be aware of the issues being challenged by the student so that they too can prepare their position and present evidence to support it. The field instructor and faculty representative may present the case, they may be assisted by the field co-ordinator, or the school may engage a lawyer.

The appeal committee hears the case and communicates its decision in writing to all participants within a set period of time. If the student is not satisfied with the outcome of the appeal there may be a higher level of appeal within the university or the student may seek a hearing in a court of law.

The following are some recurring issues that have been raised at appeals of field grades.

1. Is there sufficient evidence to support a failing grade? Written process records, project reports, audio or video tapes, and written documentation of observed student behaviours are necessary to provide examples of the lack of appropriate performance behaviours. Evaluation of these materials must be in relation to objectives of the practicum. Thus, there is a need for clearly defined behavioural objectives against which judgments can be made regarding the student's learning and practice performance. Even in the case of bizarre or inappropriate student behaviour, it is advisable to document the incident at the time it occurs and to share this notation with the student. If other personnel were involved they should be asked to document their observations and these individuals may be called as witnesses.

2. Is there agreement that the student's performance warrants a failing grade? When a failing grade is considered the field instructor and the faculty representative are expected to review the student's work. In some schools, a "second reader", a faculty member or field instructor, who does not know the student is asked to review a selection of the student's work and provide an evaluation.

3. Were regular procedures followed in field instruction that conform to the school's expectations? Was the educational contract or agreement met? That is, were the duties and expectations of the field instructor in respect to teaching the student carried out? Did the student have enough learning opportunities to master required skills? Did the student have field instruction sessions as contracted? Was the procedure in field instruction fair? That is, was the student given feedback, was the student informed of problem behaviours, were the objectives for change specified, was the student given sufficient time to make changes? Was the student informed of the possibility of failure? Was the faculty representative involved? Were the outcomes of meetings with the faculty representative clearly conveyed to the student? It is very helpful for instructors to have notes summarizing field instruction sessions, highlighting when they met, what was discussed, and what issues for change were identified. In some schools, the faculty representative takes responsibility for documenting minutes of conference meetings. These written materials may be used as evidence in an appeal to demonstrate that the student experienced fair and regular field instruction which attempted to assist the student in reaching practice competence.

Notes

1 Malcolm Knowles, "Innovations in Teaching Styles and Approaches Based Upon Adult Learning," *Journal of Education for Social Work* 8 (Spring 1972): 39.

2 Suanna J. Wilson, *Field Instruction: Techniques for Supervision* (New York: Macmillan, 1981), p. 164.

3 Alex Gitterman and Naomi Pines Gitterman, "Social Work Student Evaluation: Format and Method," *Journal of Education for Social Work* 15 (Fall 1979): 103.

4 Alfred Kadushin, *Supervision in Social Work* (New York: Columbia University Press, 1976), p. 293.

5 Wilson, *Field Instruction*, p. 164.

6 Joan Pennell, *Integration Model for Field Instruction: Training Manual* (School of Social Work, Memorial University of Newfoundland, 1980), p. 150.

7 Wilson, *Field Instruction*, p. 185.

8 E. Clifford Brennan, "Evaluation of Field Teaching and Learning," in *Quality Field Instruction in Social Work*, eds. Bradford W. Sheafor and Lowell E. Jenkins (New York: Longman, 1982), p. 81.

9 Ibid., p. 81.

10 Kadushin, *Supervision in Social Work*, p. 287.

11 Ibid, p. 290.

12 Gitterman and Gitterman, "Social Work Student Evaluation: Format and Method," p. 105.

13 Wilson, *Field Instruction*, pp. 186-192.

12 Endings

The ending of the practicum is built into its beginning. The contract made with the school and the student specifies the length of the practicum. Separations will occur at the scheduled time but, as in all relationships, such knowledge is generally denied by all parties until the actual time of parting has arrived. As the ending approaches, it is not unusual for a kind of mourning process to take over. This can be manifested by apathy in field instruction sessions, or apprehension on the part of the student at contemplating having to face the real world of employment.

If the practicum has been a satisfying experience for both student and field instructor, it is not unusual for a field instructor to say, "If only I could keep her for a while longer so she can really reinforce what she has learned." Both the student and the field instructor are feeling ambivalent. There is pleasure in the successful outcome of having established a good learning/teaching relationship and sadness that this relationship must now end. It is relatively easy for the field instructor to acknowledge this ambivalence. In some instances separation is postponed because students remain in the agency as short-term employees or may be employed on an ongoing basis. Some students and field instructors avoid separation when each has received such gratification from the relationship that they become lifelong friends and colleagues. A different and troubling situation occurs, however, when only the student wishes to continue the relationship and the field instructor does not share this need. Phone calls and lunch invitations need sensitive but honest responses. It is certainly true that field instructors can become lifetime models for students who do incorporate large parts of the professional behaviour of their field instructor.

If the practicum has been perceived as more positive by either the student or the field instructor, the acknowledgement of feelings is more difficult. Either may feel great relief that the practicum is ending and be unaware that the other is feeling the loss of an important relationship. It is helpful to review the events of field instruction sessions together, and to recall the good and bad experiences of the work. This process should be initiated by the field instructor in order to give the student permission to express feelings about the experience and about separation and ending.

It is possible for a practicum to end with the student receiving a passing grade, yet where the general tone of the field instruction relationship was unsatisfying and troubled. In this instance, field instructors may feel guilty about their part in contributing to the difficulty and may also feel some anger and resentment toward the student and the school. These feelings are more difficult to express, but they should not be glossed over in an attempt to put a neutral closure on the experience. It may be a helpful process to review the events and to pull from them whatever can be learned that might be helpful to the student and to the field instructor in working with students in the future. Both parties may feel guilty and angry and these feelings need to be explored and expressed. Field instructors should express any dissatisfaction about the role of the school to the faculty representative, the practicum co-ordinator, or the dean or director of the school.

By initiating the review of the practicum experience, the field instructor is modelling appropriate behaviour for the student to employ in helping clients, colleagues, or staff whose work with that student is also ending. Shulman observed the parallel nature of these processes which "can provide the supervisor with an opportunity to demonstrate the very skills the worker needs to employ with his or her clients."[1] The student needs to be encouraged to set the ending process in motion with clients well in advance of the actual ending date.

Ritual is frequently employed to mark the rites of separation. Field instructors can facilitate the expression of feelings about the end of the practicum not only by initiating the review of events with the student but also by noting the ending date in a meeting with other staff so that the ending phase is formally acknowledged.[2] Staff lunches, parties, or small gift exchanges are rites that provide students with a feeling of being a valued part of an organization. Ritual alone, however, tends to focus on the positive and superficial, and if this is all that marks the end of the practicum, there will be an unsatisfied feeling of unfinished business. A farewell party alone cannot take the place of careful discussion and review of the whole practicum experience.

This book will end with a look at the reader's future as a field instructor. To learn the skills of field instruction takes a significant investment of time and energy on the part of field instructors and the schools. It is clear that continued use of the skills of field instruction can serve to refine and sharpen them and can only ensure a more effective practicum and students better prepared to enter the profession. Schools have an interest, therefore, in retaining field instructors who have acquired these skills. Quality field instruction should give personal satisfaction to field instructors and should be recognized as a distinct professional practice skill by both the agency and the educational institution.

Field instructors may choose from among several options to ensure that field instruction becomes a part of their professional careers. These options include ongoing association as a master field instructor or adjunct professor with one school; alternating between two or more schools in a community as a field instructor; taking a student periodically rather than consecutively; recruiting and training agency colleagues to become field instructors and assisting the school in monitoring their progress. Schools of social work need to acknowledge the effort expended by field instructors and the importance of their contribution to social work education. Schools might consider inviting field instructors to lecture to practice classes, to participate on school committees which set educational policy, or to award adjunct faculty appointments to field instructors. In addition schools might make continuing education available to field instructors.

It requires the co-operation of academic and practice educators to produce social workers who will enhance professional knowledge and practice and address real societal need. Integration of theory and practice can serve not just students but also field and school educators.

Notes

1 Lawrence Shulman, *Skills of Supervision and Staff Management* (Itasca, Illinois: F.E. Peacock, 1982), p. 299.
2 Ibid., p. 300.

APPENDIX:
AN ANNOTATED BIBLIOGRAPHY
Compiled by Imogen Taylor, Marion Bogo, Elaine Vayda

Acknowledgements

We would like to thank the following persons for submitting bibliographies on field instruction which have been useful to the development of this annotated bibliography.

Marjory Campbell Professor, School of Social Work, Memorial University
Richard Carrière Assistant Professor, School of Social Work, Laurentian University
Barbara Cowan Professor, Faculty of Social Work, Wilfrid Laurier University
Sandra de Vink Assistant Professor, Department of Social Work, St. Thomas University
Nancy Dickson Instructor, School of Social Work, University of British Columbia
Sheila Goldbloom Associate Professor, School of Social Work, McGill University
Kenneth Gordon Associate Professor, Department of Social Work, King's College, University of Western Ontario
Jack Kugelmass Manager, Social Work Department, Toronto General Hospital
Mary MacLean Assistant Professor, School of Social Work, Carleton University
Jackie Pace Lecturer, Maritime School of Social Work, Dalhousie University
Elizabeth Pittaway Co-ordinator of Field Instruction, Department of Social Work, King's College, University of Western Ontario
Ruth Rachlis Lecturer, School of Social Work, University of Manitoba
Melanie Waite Assistant Professor, Department of Social Work, Lakehead University

We would also like to thank Felicity Coulter for her invaluable assistance and patience in preparing this bibliography.

Introduction

There is a substantial body of field instruction literature and literature specific to supervision of students, but there is comparatively minimal reference to the issue of how field instructors or student supervisors acquire the skills necessary to carry out their role competently and effectively.

This annotated review is intended to introduce the reader to literature related to the issue of field instructor training and all this comprises. As there is minimal literature which focuses specifically on field instructor training the majority of references here address related areas. References are drawn primarily from social work field instruction literature with some reference to social work supervision, training, and education literature.

To enable the reader to locate particular items of interest annotations are classified into sections, each one bearing a particular relationship to field instructor training. Introductory comments to each section describe criteria for selection as well as identify apparent "gaps" in the literature. Classification was completed on the basis of the component of the reference deemed most relevant to the topic of field instructor training. Annotations appear in full in the category where they are most relevant; they may be cross-referenced once only to a secondary classification. As with all classification systems there is not always a perfect fit.

Material was reviewed from journals, books and reports published since 1970 in Canada and the United States. Particularly relevant pre-1970 'classics' have also been included. All unpublished Canadian work submitted to the F.I.T. Project is annotated. Relevant Canadian doctoral dissertations are also annotated.

An alphabetical 'Author Index' accompanies the Annotated Bibliography, referring only to those titles which have been annotated.

History of Field Instruction

Discussion of the history of field instruction as an integral part of social work education occurs infrequently in the field instruction literature compared to discussion of the history of social work supervision. One author (George, 1982) specifically traces themes and changes in the content and method of field instruction since its inception.

1.
George, A. "A History of Social Work Field Instruction." In **Quality Field Instruction in Social Work,** pp. 37-59. Edited by B.W. Sheafor and L.E. Jenkins. New York: Longman, 1982.

An historical perspective is given on the emergence of field instruction as an essential part of social work education. The use of an apprenticeship model in training "friendly visitors" in the pre-1900 Charity Organization Societies is traced through to present patterns in social work education. Also discussed in relation to field instruction are the emergence of accreditation standards, the influential role of field placement agencies, the influence of various schools of thought and the development of method specialties.

2.
Kutzik, A.J. "History and Philosophy of Supervision and Consultation: The Social Work Field." In **Supervision, Consultation & Staff Training in the Helping Professions,** pp. 25-29. Edited by F.W. Kaslow and Associates. San Francisco: Jossey-Bass, 1977.

A detailed description of the history and philosophy of supervision and consultation particularly focusing on the confusion which at times exists between the two processes. It is suggested that "supervision" of experienced professional social workers is essentially consultative and to identify it as such would strengthen social work practice in host settings by recognizing the autonomy of the professional social worker.

Wijnberg, M.H. and M.C. Schwartz. Models of student supervision: The apprentice, growth, and role systems models. Journal of Education for Social Work, 13(3): 107-113, 1977. See *Approaches to Field Instruction,* #53 for annotation.

Definitions of Field Instruction

With the exception of one author (Dastyk-Blackmore, 1982) there appear to be no significant attempts to distil the essence of field instruction and compare and contrast it to social work supervision. Both field instruction and social work supervisory literature appear to assume the processes are similar and inter-related, hence the confusion in nomenclature.

3.
Dastyk-Blackmore, R. Is field teaching supervision? Canadian Journal of Social Work Education, 8(3): 75-80, 1982.

The interchangeable use of terms such as 'supervision' and 'field instructor' reflects confusion about the nature and objectives of field education and the roles of both students and teachers. It is suggested that although there are similarities, there are also significant conceptual differences between field teaching and supervision. In order to facilitate the shift from identifying the field solely with work experience, factors such as the objectives and functions of field teachers and supervisors, differences in levels and areas of competence, and differences in relationships and accountability are discussed. Until the similarities and differences are understood, social work education will continue to have difficulty in developing appropriate field experiences for students.

Matorin, S. Dimensions of student supervision: A point of view. Social Casework, 60(3): 150-156, 1979. See *The Instructional Relationship,* #60 for annotation.

4.
Murdaugh, J. Brief notes: Student supervision unbound. Social Work, 19(2): 131-132, 1974.

Different approaches to the role of student supervision are briefly described. Contracting as a means to mutual accountability is recommended. Appropriate role titles are discussed and the terms student and mentor recommended.

Field Instructor Training

The notion of field instructor training is relatively recent and with the exception of two authors (Bogo, 1981; Hersh, 1984) it is referred to only in passing in referenced field instruction literature, often in the form of descriptions of the role of field co-ordinator or recommendations to faculties. The notion of social work supervisors needing to learn skills to instruct and manage staff is also relatively recent although it is addressed more frequently in the social work supervision literature hence some references in this section.

5.
Akin, G. & Weil, M. The prior question: How do supervisors learn to supervise? Social Casework, 62(8): 472-79, 1981.

Little research has been done to document how supervisors learn the skills needed to instruct and manage staff. Seven basic processes discussed in the literature which are assumed to produce effective supervision are identified: 1) role adoption, 2) emulation or modelling, 3) reframing current skills, 4) acquisition of new skills, 5) formal education—role preparation, 6) exhortation or prescription, and 7) selection. Lacking research, it is unclear how useful these processes are in increasing the effectiveness of supervisory development. Work is needed to develop and test models of supervisory learning and to assess what process and content prepare supervisors for competent practice.

Bogo, M. Field instruction: Negotiating content and process. Clinical Supervisor, 1(3): 3-13, 1983. See *Learning Theories*, #32, for annotation.

6.
Bogo, M. An educationally focused faculty/field liaison program for first-time field instructors. Journal of Education for Social Work, 17(3): 59-65, 1981. See *Learning Theories*, p. 12 for cross-reference.

Regular small group meetings for liaison between field and faculty have been used to provide new field instructors with knowledge and skill in learning and teaching in the practicum. Through use of an andragogical model, this new knowledge can be used in the instructor's current experience as a field practice educator. In addition, linkages between field and faculty are strengthened, a mutual aid group is developed to facilitate carrying a new role, and the group provides a mechanism for achieving greater uniformity in interpretation of student performance expectations.

Gordon, M.S. "Responsibilities of the School." In **Quality Field Instruction in Social Work**, pp. 116-135. Edited by B.W. Sheafor and L.E. Jenkins. New York: Longman, 1982. See *Context for Field Instruction*, #17, for annotation.

7.
Hawkins, F.R. & Pennell, J. "Training for Field Instructor Competence: Utilization of an Integration Model". Memorial University of Newfoundland, 1983. Unpublished Paper.

This paper presents the rationale and constructs the parameters of an integration model of field instruction which was used in a training program for field instructors at Memorial University of Newfoundland. The findings of a research study to determine the effects of this training as program participation are reported. The implications of this research are discussed in terms of social work education and field instructor training.

Henry, C. St. G. An examination of field work models at Adelphi University School of Social Work. Journal of Education for Social Work, 11(3): 62-68, 1975. See *Context for Field Instruction, #18*, for annotation.

8.
Hersh, A. Teaching the theory and practice of student supervision: A short-term model based on principles of adult education. The Clinical Supervisor, 2(1): 29-44, 1984.

The learning of the theory and practice of student supervision is discussed, utilizing an adult education model. A course outline is described providing a sequencing of content and focus based on prior understanding of the student learning process, including the time structure; and an understanding of the supervisor's learning style and need to master the "basics" of supervision.

9.
Krop, L.P. Developing and evaluating a training manual for social work field instructors using elements of the behaviouristic system of learning. Arlington, VA.: ERIC Document Reproduction Service, 1975.

A major problem in social work field education is that there is very little organized structure or order to field teaching. This document discusses the creation and evaluation of a training manual in performance-oriented field instruction that can be used as a tool for field instructors to develop an orderly and systematic progression of teaching. Behavioural learning theory is utilized. The manual is designed as a self-instructional guide for field instructors to prepare instructional units for students and develop a curriculum for field work.

10.
Krop, L.P. A strategy for obtaining a performance-oriented training program for social work field instructors. Arlington, VA.: ERIC Document Reproduction Service, 1975.

The development and implementation of a performance-oriented training program for field instructors is presented. An initial survey of the needs of field instructors is described together with the strategy designed and implemented to engage the support of the school. The content and format of the program, including tools and strategies for field instruction, is briefly outlined.

Context for Field Instruction

The School of Social Work, University, and Profession are of particular significance in reviewing the context of field instruction. The question of whether field practice occurs within an urban or rural environment is significant although as most field instruction literature tends to assume practice in urban settings, only the literature specific to rural communities is reviewed here.

School of Social Work; University; Field

Field instruction occurs at the interface of these institutions and each has a differing mandate, orientation, and time frame. The literature reflects considerable interest in the interaction of the different communities and the resulting impact on field personnel.

11.
Campbell, M. "Consultation – The Essential Link in Social Work Field Programmes." School of Social Work, Memorial University. Unpublished Paper.

The role of the field consultant in a school of social work's field practicum is of critical importance yet feedback from Canadian instructors criticizes faculties for the lack of attention given to this aspect of the field program. The consultation process requires long-term planning as well as administrative support. Field co-ordinators and faculty liaisons need sufficient time to identify the consultation needs of agency settings and to develop a contract with field instructors. Factors such as the years of experience of the field instructor, the student's performance, the stance of the agency's administrator and staff viz a viz student placements, and student work assignments, influence the type of consultation required. Schools of social work that take the initiative in becoming responsive to the consultation needs of field instructors will provide enrichment to the field instructor, student, and school.

12.
Cohen, J. Selected constraints in the relationship between social work education and practice. Journal of Education for Social Work, 13(1): 3-7, 1977.

The gap between graduate social work education and practice has long been identified as an issue of concern to both groups as well as to the professional organizations with which they are affiliated. Differences exist with respect to: 1) view of professionalism in social work; 2) structural constraints, in particular the different 'audiences' to which each group must relate in addition to having to relate to each other; 3) time perspectives, where practice must respond to relatively immediate problems and needs while educators and researchers take a more long-term perspective; and 4) autonomy, where there is comparatively little practitioner autonomy compared with other professions yet faculty maintain 'the sanctity of academic freedom.' It is suggested that rather than limiting the natural differentiation of practice and education the creative force of each may add to a professional vitality.

13.
Cowan, B. & Wickham, E. Field teaching in university context. Canadian Journal of Social Work Education, 8(3): 81-86, 1982.

Field teaching in professional social work education requires the development of sound theoretical principles to guide practice. A partnership between university and practice setting is necessary for the field teaching process to be effective. The partnership should include clear contractual arrangements regarding: selection of field teachers and field practice setting; time allotted to practice; curriculum objectives; responsibilities of field teacher and field setting; role of the university; criteria for evaluation of student performance; guidelines for problem situations; agency resources for student practice; liability and malpractice insurance coverage. Such a partnership will be conducive to student learning.

14.
Dea, K. "The Collaborative Process in Undergraduate Field Instruction." In **Undergraduate Field Instruction Programs: Current Issues and Predictions,** pp. 50-62. Edited by K. Wenzel. New York: Council on Social Work Education, 1972.

Traditional field instruction patterns of university, agency and mutually directed programs are reviewed from a historical perspective. Collaborative relationships based on a transactional model of field instruction are strongly encouraged by the author for more effective field instruction. Fiscal, academic, philosophical, role, political and community restraints to the development of collaborative relationships between schools of social work and agencies are presented.

15.
Fellin, P.A. "Responsibilities of the School." In **Quality Field Instruction in Social Work,** p. 101-116. Edited by B.W. Sheafor and L.E. Jenkins. New York: Longman, 1982.

The function of the school, and dean or program director, in providing adequate resources and giving personal leadership to the field instruction enterprise is examined. This involves seeking sanction from the university and maintaining sound working relationships with the practice community. It also involves finding an approach to field instruction compatible with objectives and resources of the program, and providing adequate staffing within a sound organizational structure.

16.
Frumkin, M. Social work education and the professional commitment fallacy: A practical guide to field-school relations. Journal of Education for Social Work, 16(2): 91-99, 1980.

Open systems and exchange theory is utilized to develop a framework for analyzing school-agency relationships. The framework is composed of: 1) a review of the underlying dynamics of school-agency relationships, and 2) an evaluation of the intra-organizational and environmental factors that influence the relationships. An overall strategy for guiding the development of school-agency relationships is presented.

Gitterman, A. "The Faculty Field Instructor in Social Work Education." In **The Dynamics of Field Instruction,** pp. 31-39. New York: Council on Social Work Education, 1975. See *Research Studies in Field Instruction,* #134 for annotation.

17.
Gordon, M.S. "Responsibilities of the School." In **Quality Field Instruction in Social Work,** pp. 116-135. Edited by B.W. Sheafor and L.E. Jenkins. New York: Longman, 1982. See *Field Instructor Training,* p. 4 for cross-reference.

Responsibilities of the school for maintenance of the field program are described, including the role of the faculty field liaison. Supports are identified which the school might offer to help the field instructor become a good teacher. School-agency relationships are discussed. A suggested outline for a field instruction manual is provided.

18.
Henry, C. St. G. An examination of field work models at Adelphi University School of Social Work. Journal of Education for Social Work, 11(3): 62-68, 1975. See *Field Instructor Training*, p. 5, for cross-reference.

The philosophy, conceptual framework and operationalization of models of field work education at Adelphi University School of Social Work are described, together with examples of different kinds of practicum settings. The administrative, consultative and educational functions of the practicum co-ordinator are outlined. As educator, the co-ordinator conducts bi-weekly seminars with field instructors, teaching them how to develop educational assessment of students. Identifying students' learning style, pace of learning, problems in learning and learning plateaus are discussed.

Jenkins, L.E. & Sheafor, B.W. "An Overview of Social Work Field Instruction." In **Quality Field Instruction in Social Work,** pp. 3-20. Edited by B.W. Sheafor and L.E. Jenkins. New York: Longman, 1982. See *Approaches to Field Instruction*, #49 for annotation.

19.
Jones, E.F. Square peg, round hole: The dilemma of the undergraduate social work field coordinator. Journal of Education for Social Work 20(3): 45-50, 1984.

Some of the difficulties faced by the field work co-ordinator in professional baccalaureate social work programs are reviewed. Particularly important is the lack of recognition by academic executives of the administrative-co-ordinative-educative performance expectations. It is suggested that the role definitions and responsibilities set out by the 1971 Council on Social Work Education be clarified and broadly disseminated to social work faculty, program directors, practitioners, and non-social work administrators.

Kimberley, M.D. & Watt, S. Trends and issues in the field preparation of social work manpower: Part III: Educational policy, accreditation standards, and guidelines. Canadian Journal of Social Work Education, 8(1 & 2): 101-120, 1982. See *Research Studies in Field Instruction*, #136 for annotation.

20.
Krop, L.P. Developing and implementing effective modes of communication between the school of social work and agency-based faculty. Arlington, VA.: ERIC Document Reproduction Service, 1975.

If the field instructional agency is to be an educationally focused learning experience for the student, operative school-agency communication must be established. The process of reviewing and revising methods of communication is described with the goal of enabling field instructors to: 1) achieve a better relationship with the school, 2) integrate class and field teaching, 3) give teaching roles greater priority, and 4) participate more actively in the governance of the school.

21.
Rosenblum, A.F. & Raphael, F.B. The role and function of the faculty-field liaison. Journal of Education for Social Work, 19(1): 67-73, 1983.

An attempt is made to examine the purposes, define the role and analyze the functions of a faculty-field liaison. The experience of faculty members who have carried this assignment as a major responsibility is described. Recognizing the impact of this role on the educational process, an attempt is made to distill its essence and clarify the requirements for effective practice.

22.
Rothman, J. Development of a profession: Field instructor correlates. Social

Service Review, 51(2): 289-310, 1977. See *Field – Class Integration*, p. 19, for cross-reference.

Field instruction in social work is discussed with reference to the development and maturation of professions. The premise is that professions go through phases as they develop starting with heavy reliance on the field for practice skill acquisition, proceeding to an equal sharing between the field and the university, and culminating in the assumption of major responsibility by the university. It is suggested that social work is in the middle phase. Professional maturation will require increased responsibility by schools of social work for the transmission of the skills of practice to students. Various approaches and formats to achieve this are discussed and diverse training methods, including service and training centers and skills' laboratories, are described.

23.
Schutz, M.L. & Gordon, W.E. Reallocation of educational responsibility among schools, agencies, students and NASW. Journal of Education for Social Work, 13(2): 99-106, 1977.

Graduate social work schools are failing as gatekeepers to the profession. Variation in admission, course and grade requirements, with accountability left to the schools in certifying the beginning practice level, is regarded as highly dysfunctional. The writers, utilizing a comptency-based approach, propose that schools prepare for practice, after which agencies accredited by the profession would teach the student to practice, with final certification of competence in practice resting with a public-based licensure board. This rearrangement will produce accountability that should improve teaching, learning, and practice.

24.
Sheafor, B.W. & Jenkins, L.E. Issues that affect the development of a field instruction curriculum. Journal of Education for Social Work, 17(1): 12-20, 1981. See *Approaches to Field Instruction*, p. 16, for cross-reference.

Several of the factors that influence the construction of a field instruction curriculum, and that should be considered when developing a curriculum, are identified and examined. These include: the influence of the profession, university, region, and students; the teaching-learning process; and three distinct approaches to field instruction commonly found in social work education, specifically, the apprenticeship, academic, and articulated approaches. The factors are then appraised with respect to their cost to the school and the field placement agency, and their impact on educational outcomes.

Thomlison, B. & Watt, S. Trends and issues in the field preparation of social work manpower: A summary report. Canadian Journal of Social Work Education, 6(2 & 3): 137-158, 1980. See *Research Studies in Field Instruction*, #148 for annotation.

25.
Tropman, E.J. Agency constraints affecting links between practice and education. Journal of Education for Social Work, 13(1): 8-14, 1977. See *Teaching/Learning Methodology*, p. 22, for cross-reference.

Education and practice are closely interrelated and interdependent. There are, however, inherent constraints within agencies that complicate or interfere with the achievement of an ideal relationship. These relate to such factors as the history and culture of the agency, its structure and funding pattern, its commitment to the educational task, the qualifications of its staff for the educational function, the attitude of its staff toward partners in the educational venture, the demands on it for service, and the confidential and political aspects of some of its operations.

Watt, S. & Kimberley, M.D. Trends and issues in the field preparation of social work manpower: Part II, policies and recommendations. Canadian Journal of Social Work Education, 7(1): 99-108, 1981. See *Research Studies in Field Instruction*, #149 for annotation.

Rural Environment

References here address the issue particularly of field practice in rural areas. Because of the relative paucity of field instruction literature on this issue references have also been drawn from literature pertaining to social work supervision, training, and continuing education in rural areas.

26.
De Jong, C.R. "Field Instruction for Undergraduate Social Work Education in Rural Areas." In **The Dynamics of Field Instruction**, pp. 20-30. New York: Council on Social Work Education, 1975.

The question is addressed of whether social workers who practice in rural settings need special skills and knowledge not required for practice in urban settings. Changes in traditional teaching methods and organizational structure of field instruction are presented as necessary for the preparation of generalist practitioners. An example is given of the development of a specific field instruction program.

27.
Horejsi, C.R. & Deaton, R.L. The cracker-barrel classroom: Rural programming for continuing education. Journal of Education for Social Work, 13(3): 37-43, 1977.

Any consideration of problems and issues in programming for continuing education in a rural area must logically begin with an overview of physical and demographic factors common to the region. Characteristics of rural social work practice and of human service organizations in small communities should also be considered. Educational resources are scarce in rural areas; shared sponsorship and interagency collaboration are often necessary in the development of educational programs. Innovation is needed in the use of teaching materials.

28.
Markowski, E.M. & Cain, H.I. Marital and family therapy training and supervision: A regional model for rural mental health. The Clinical Supervisor, 1(1): 65-75, 1983.

It has been difficult and sometimes impossible for therapists in rural areas to obtain training and supervision in marital and family therapy outside the community mental health centres in which they are employed. Presented is a regional program that focuses on training and supervision in marital and family therapy. Judged successful by the planners, supervisors, and participants, the program is an example of the way in which the creative pooling of resources can help to meet the training and supervision needs of rural mental health workers.

29.
Weber, G.K. Preparing social workers for practice in rural social systems. Journal of Education for Social Work, 12(3): 108-15, 1976.

Schools of social work should provide more workers for practice in rural settings. The basic character of rural areas and the need for systematic intervention and program development to alter the disproportionate amount of social and economic problems existing there are discussed. The use of rural settings for student practice is reviewed, including: concepts such as the community of communities; models for designing practice experiences; the role of the educator; and positive features and barriers found in providing social services.

Teaching/Learning Transactions

The majority of references in this annotated bibliography relate to teaching/ learning transactions between field instructor and student. An attempt is made here to introduce sub-categories, recognizing, nevertheless, that categories are inter-related and cannot be mutually exclusive.

Learning Theories

In particular references regarding adult education, competency-based education, and learning styles are selected for inclusion here on the basis of their direct relevance for field instruction. Specific learning theories such as cognitive and behavioural theories are not reviewed. These theories are available if the reader is interested.

30.
Arkava, M. & Brennen, E.C. eds., Competency-Based Education for Social Work: Evaluation and Curriculum Issues. New York: Council on Social Work Education, 1976. See *Educational Strategies*, p. 23, for cross-reference.

In response to the need for accountability in social work education, the authors review assessment efforts including knowledge and value inventories, skill assessment scales, and simulation models. Three separate attempts to appraise student competence are reviewed. The University of Montana's experience in assessing practice skills of baccalaureate social work students in practicum settings is reviewed and evaluated.

31.
Berengarten, S. Identifying learning patterns of individual students: An exploratory study. Social Service Review, 31(4): 407-417, 1957.

An empirical study was undertaken to identify the learning patterns of sixteen first and second year students from a variety of field settings. Students' learning was characterized in three main sub-patterns, the experiential-empathic learner, the doer, and the intellectual-empathic. Seven major areas were then systematically studied in the light of the sub-patterns: the students selective response to learning demands; responsibility and use of supervision in learning; the timing, quality and handling of anxiety; the quality of conceptualization and use of previous experience; stimuli associated with positive learning experiences; the time pattern; and performance qualities. A relationship is drawn between teaching patterns and student learning behaviour.

32.
Bogo, M. Field instruction: Negotiating content and process. Clinical Supervisor, 1(3): 3-13, 1983. See *Field Instructor Training*, p. 4, for cross-reference.

Contemporary professional practice necessitates continuous education and development. Social work practicum education needs to develop practice competence, responsibility and expertise in self-directed learning in students. Practicum structures emphasizing student participation in selection and negotiation of the content and process of the learning/teaching enterprise will facilitate achievement of this educational goal.

Bogo, M. An educationally focused faculty/field liaison program for first-time field instructors. Journal of Education for Social Work, 17(3): 59-65, 1981. See *Field Instructor Training*, #6 for annotation.

33.
Clancy, C. The use of the andragogical approach in the educational function of supervision in social work. The Clinical Supervisor, 3(1): 75-86, 1985.

Knowles' andragogical approach to the education of adults is applied to the educational function of supervision in social work. The four underlying assumptions of andragogy: self concept, experience, readiness to learn, and time perspective and orientation to learning are discussed briefly. Knowles' seven steps of the andragogical process are related to the process of supervision in social work. The personal/ interpersonal and organizational advantages and disadvantages of this approach are discussed.

34.
Claxton, C.S. & Ralston, Y. Learning Styles: Their Impact on Teaching and Administration. Washington, D.C.: American Association for Higher Education, 1978.

In Part I of this monograph several models of learning styles are described and the major implications of these models for college and university teaching are discussed. In Part II the impact that instructional change has on the student, the instructor, and the institution is reviewed.

35.
Dwyer, M. & Urbanowski, M. Field Practice criteria: A valuable teaching/ learning tool in undergraduate social work education. Journal of Education for Social Work, 17(1): 5-11, 1981.

Criteria that identify and describe the expected performance levels of undergraduate social work students should be clearly stated. These criteria should be an integral part of the field work program and reflect the social work program's goals and objectives, the needs of the community's social service delivery systems, and the standards on accreditation. They should be a helpful tool to both students and field instructors in assuming mutual responsibilities for learning and teaching, and in reaching their respective goals.

36.
Eisikovits, Z. & Guttman, E. Toward a practice theory of learning through experience in social work supervision. The Clinical Supervisor, 1(1): 51-63, 1983.

Dewey's experiential educational theory is used to conceptualize the learning component of social work supervision and to introduce a model of learning through experience in supervision. Each of the five components of the model emerges from the other. The components are: 1) placement of the supervisee in a demanding reality context; 2) emergence of the supervisee's need to learn and to master new, applied skills; 3) use of newly acquired skills in responsible challenging action; 4) opportunities for critical analysis and reflection and formation of abstractions, principles, and generalizations. Each component is briefly discussed, as is the viability of this practice theory model for learning through supervision.

Gelfand, B., Rohrich, S., Nevidon, P. & Starak, I. An andragogical application to the training of social workers. Journal of Education for Social Work, 11(3): 55-61, 1975. See *Research Studies in Field Instruction*, #133 for annotation.

37.

Gitterman, A. "Comparison of Educational Models and Their Influences on Supervision." In **Issues in Human Services,** pp. 18-38. Edited by F.W. Kaslow and Associates. San Francisco: Jossey-Bass, 1972.

Three models of education: the subject-centred, student-centred and integrative models, are interrelated with three models of social work supervision: the organization-centred, worker-centred, and integrative models. The integrative model is recommended where the process of learning and doing is presented as active and purposeful, and where both teacher and learner have a major function to perform. The outcome of their joint contribution is greater than their individual combinations.

38.

Gitterman, A. & Miller, I. "Supervisors as Educators." In **Supervision, Consultation, and Staff Training in the Helping Professions,** pp. 100-114. Edited by F.W. Kaslow and Associates. San Francisco: Jossey-Bass, 1977.

Theory and skill about how to instruct others has received minimal attention. The authors identify basic concepts pertinent to achieving balance between content and process, or learner and subject, drawing particularly on the work of John Dewey. The following concepts are elaborated on: operationalization, generalization, recreating, peer learning, and role modelling. Case illustrations are used to show the supervisor as educator helping the worker with practice dilemmas.

39.

Kettner, P.M. A conceptual framework for developing learning modules for field education. Journal of Education for Social Work, 15(1): 51-58, 1979.

Since the beginning of social work education, field education has been considered a vital component of every social work program, yet social work educators have for the most part been unwilling to commit themselves to a specific set of objectives in field education. The purposes of a study were: to determine the level of specificity of objectives and content achieved in field education programs; to analyze the structure and function of monitoring and evaluation systems; and to propose a framework for modularizing field education content that will achieve a high degree of precision in its teaching and learning.

40.

Knowles, M.S. Innovations in teaching styles and approaches based upon adult learning. Journal of Education for Social Work, 8(2): 32-39, 1972.

Differences in assumptions about learning of pedagogy (teaching children) and andragogy (helping adults learn) are examined. The implications of these differences for: program planning, the design of learning experiences, the selection of methods and techniques, and evaluation are reviewed. The suggestion is made that social work education, which has traditionally been pedagogically oriented, is dealing with essentially mature students whose learning would be enhanced by application of principles and techniques of andragogy. Differences between the two approaches are discussed in four main areas: changes in self-concept; the role of experience; readiness to learn; and orientation to learning. A process design based on mutual, self-directed inquiry is presented.

41.

Kolb, D.A. Experiential Learning: Experience as the Source of Learning and Development. Englewood Cliffs, New Jersey: Prentice-Hall, Inc., 1984.

A systematic statement of the theory of experiential learning and its application to education, work, and adult development. Drawing from the works of John Dewey,

Kurt Lewin, and Jean Piaget, this book describes the process of experiential learning and proposes a model of the underlying structure of the learning process. This structural model leads to a typology of individual learning styles and corresponding structures of knowledge in different disciplines, professions, and careers. The developmental focus of the book is based on the thesis that experience is the process whereby human development occurs.

Larsen, J. & Hepworth, D. Enhancing the effectiveness of practicum instruction: An empirical study. Journal of Education for Social Work, 18(2): 50-58, 1980. See *Research Studies in Field Instruction,* #138 for annotation.

42.
Larsen, J. Competency-based and task-centred practicum instruction. Journal of Education for Social Work, 16(1): 87-94, 1980. See *Educational Strategies*, p. 24, for cross-reference.

Competency-based education is an emerging and promising form of instruction for the teaching and learning of specific social work skills. Eight interpersonal skills are identified and clearly defined, along with task-centred instructional techniques, for facilitating student mastery of these skills.

43.
Lowy, L. Social work supervision: From models toward theory. Journal of Education for Social Work, 19(2): 55-62, 1983.

Among the various models of supervision in social work, the learning-oriented model emphasizes supervision as a learning and teaching process. The major learning theories on which this model is based are reviewed, including learning through discovery, affective theories of learning, and behaviour modification. It is suggested that supervision needs to be eclectic in fashioning an integrative approach to learning. Additional aspects of supervision are discussed including adult education principles, supervision as a change process, and phases of supervision. The impact of organizational and administrative variables are briefly reviewed.

44.
Matching Teaching & Learning Styles. Theory Into Practice, Winter, 1984.

This journal includes a series of papers which focus primarily on recent theory regarding teaching and learning styles. The papers address the field of education and, in particular, the classroom setting. Of some relevance to field instruction in social work are those papers on: matching styles (Henson and Borthwick); matching learning and teaching styles (Hyman and Rosoff); applying the principles of learning/teaching style theory (Friedman and Alley); and the role of discomfort in learning (Joyce).

45.
Morton, T.D. & Kurtz, P.D. Educational supervision: A learning theory approach. Social Casework, 61(4): 240-246, 1980. See *Teaching/Learning Methodology*, p.22 for cross-reference.

The educational role of the supervisor can be enhanced through application of current research and theory on learning. Assessment, which includes: determining learning needs and performance outcomes, planning the learning experience, arranging conditions and strategies for optimal learning, and implementation of the learning plan, are discussed. Feedback on performance confirms the learner's progress and reinforces positive changes in the supervisee's capabilities.

46.
Price, H.G. Achieving a balance between self-directed and required learning. Journal of Education for Social Work, 12(1): 105-112, 1976.

In the future professional schools will include required content, not required courses, in their curricula. Adult learners will plan and design their own courses. For the present, neither educator, nor students are prepared for what Knowles calls "an andragogical experience." Meanwhile, a balance is required between knowledge and responsibility deemed essential by the school and that which the learner considers important. If such a balance can be achieved, professional education will continue to move forward in self-directed learning.

47.
Rothman, B. Perspectives on learning and teaching in continuing education. Journal of Education for Social Work, 9(2): 39-52, 1973. See *Approaches to Field Instruction*, p. 15, for cross-reference.

Concepts from contemporary education theory and practice are brought together to examine the problems and potentials in the learning-teaching situation. Teaching methodology consists of: the integration and management of the nature of the students, the stylistic strategy used by the teacher, the objectives of the learning experience, the context in which learning takes place, and the content and nature of what is to be learned. Knowledge shares with process a central position in generating and sustaining learning.

Siporin, M. "The Process of Field Instruction." In **Quality Field Instruction in Social Work,** pp. 175-197. Edited by B.W. Sheafor and L.E. Jenkins. New York: Longman, 1982. See *Approaches to Field Instruction, #50* for annotation.

48.
Somers, M.L. Contributions of learning and teaching theories to the explication of the role of the teacher in social work education. Journal of Education for Social Work, 5(2): 61-73, 1979.

Major facets of the role of teacher, and assumptions regarding learning and teaching are examined. Major concepts from learning and teaching theories are discussed as they are relevant to the learning-teaching transaction. This includes: a look at goal development; an examination of S-R theory, cognitive theory, and motivation and personality theory; and a discussion of the models of problem-solving and reflective learning and teaching.

Approaches to Field Instruction
References are included to what are variously identified in the literature as approaches and models.

Annett, A. & Pace, J. "A Consultative-Instructional Approach in Field Teaching." Faculty of Social Work, Wilfrid Laurier University, 1983. Unpublished Thesis. See *Research Studies in Field Instruction, #128* for annotation.

49.
Jenkins, L.E. & Sheafor, B.W. "An Overview of Social Work Field Instruction." In **Quality Field Instruction in Social Work,** pp. 3-20. Edited by B.W. Sheafor and L.E. Jenkins. New York: Longman, 1982. See *Context for Field Instruction*, p. 8, for cross-reference.

Field instruction is defined; its place in social work education and the several factors involved are examined. Three approaches to field instruction are discussed: the apprenticeship approach, the academic approach, and the articulated approach. The implications of each approach are analyzed.

Rothman, B. Perspectives on learning and teaching in continuing education. Journal of Education for Social Work, 9(2): 39-52, 1973. See *Learning Theories, #47* for annotation.

Sheafor, B.W & L.E. Jenkins. Issues that affect the development of a field instruction curriculum. Journal of Education for Social Work, 17(1): 12-20, 1981. See *Context for Field Instruction*, #24 for annotation.

50.
Siporin, M. "The Process of Field Instruction." In **Quality Field Instruction in Social Work**, pp. 175-197. Edited by B.W. Sheafor and L.E. Jenkins. New York: Longman, 1982. See *Learning Theories*, p. 15, for cross-reference.

Field education is a "teaching-learning process" in which there is interdependence between teacher and learner. This process is directed toward helping the student change into a competent professional social worker. The process is similar to problem-solving models used in social work practice; it includes identification of teaching-learning objectives, of teacher-student tasks, and of the phases of the teaching-learning process. The structure of the process and achievement of learning tasks depend on the centrality of the teaching-student relationship. A number of generic teaching principles, applicable to a range of field instruction settings, are identified. In following these principles the field instructor attains greater assurance of an effective outcome for the teaching-learning process.

51.
Somers, M.L. **Dimensions and dynamics of engaging the learner.** Journal of Education for Social Work, 7(3): 49-57, 1971.

The process of engaging the learner requires the teacher to deal with two major facets of the mutual enterprise: the knowledge component and the teaching-learning transaction. The latter includes the individual learner; group dimensions; characteristics of the social system and functioning of the teaching-learning unit; and the teacher who carries responsibility for the current and changing body of knowledge and his/her work with the group as a group.

52.
Webb, N.B. **Developing competent clinical practitioners: A model with guidelines for supervisors.** The Clinical Supervisor, 1(4): 41-53, 1983.

Fostering competence in clinical practitioners is a goal easier stated than accomplished. This article translates selected concepts from ego psychology and communications theory into specific guidelines for developing competent clinical practitioners. The "life model" approach to supervision presented emphasizes building from the strengths of the supervisee and promoting growth in a nurturing, supportive supervisory environment.

53.
Wijnberg, M.H. & M.C. Schwartz. **Models of student supervision: The apprentice, growth, and role systems models.** Journal of Education for Social Work, 13(3): 107-113, 1977. See *History of Field Instruction*, p. 2, for cross-reference.

The history of apprentice, growth, and role systems models of supervision is traced. Examples from field instruction are used to illustrate the impact of the models on supervisory behaviour. Learning in field work is significantly related to the manner in which the role system is defined. The structure and process of the role systems model are identified and discussed, as are its three components —communication, role expectations and performance, and mechanisms of control. It is believed that this model exerts a critical influence on students' learning.

The Instructional Relationship: Particular Dimensions
Dimensions such as styles of field instruction; empathy in instructional relationships; self-awareness of the student and field instructor; games played by student and field

instructor; issues of authority, dependency, transference and counter-transference are included here.

Amacher, K.A. Exploration into the dynamics of learning in field work. Smith College Studies in Social Work, 46(3): 163-217, 1976. See *Research Studies in Field Instruction*, #127 for annotation.

54.

Barnat, M.R. Student reactions to the first supervisory year: Relationship and resolutions. Journal of Education for Social Work, 9(3): 3-8, 1973.

The first supervisory year is examined from the standpoint of the student. Intensive, supervised experience has a powerful impact on the student. The impact is seen in three relationship areas: therapist stereotype, supervisor, and client. When the impact is positive it involves progression from greater to lesser anxiety, lesser to greater self-esteem, a peer relationship with supervisor, and tolerance for client demands.

55.

Dean, R.G. The role of empathy in supervision. Clinical Social Work Journal, 12(2): 129-139, 1984.

Empathy plays an important role in clinical supervision. It is the link between the client, the supervisee, and the supervisor. The supervisor uses an empathic capacity as well as theoretical knowledge to understand the clinical work and build the supervisory relationship. Often the progress of a case can be traced through the development of empathic understanding in supervision. The transmission of empathy requires creativity and openness and is one of the major challenges in supervision. By analyzing the different uses of empathy in clinical supervision we can increase our understanding of the supervisory process.

56.

Gizynski, M. Self awareness of the supervisor in supervision. Clinical Social Work Journal, 6(3): 202-210, 1978.

Teaching self awareness is an important and sensitive task in the supervision of the clinical casework student. However, lack of self awareness on the part of the supervisor may lead to a serious infraction of this learning experience, and there is no institutionalized process for reviewing lack of supervisory self awareness as there is for students. Some occasions in which problems of supervisory self awareness are likely to occur are: the supervisor who has difficulty responding appropriately to the student's dependency demands in supervision; the supervisor who is threatened by students whose character styles are very different from his/her own; and the supervisor who views client behaviour from the perspective of a value system very different from the student's.

57.

Hawthorne, L. Games supervisors play. Social Work, 20(3): 179-181, 1975.

Games used by supervisors to deal with problems handling the authority aspect of their role are discussed. The games are divided into two categories, "games of abdication" and "games of power", which use almost opposite strategies but are aimed at the same result: the avoidance of a clear definition and exercise of supervisory authority. The supervisee's acquiescence in these games and possible responses and counter games are also discussed.

Kadushin, A. Supervisor-supervisee: A survey. Social Work, 19(3): 288-297, 1974. See *Research Studies in Field Instruction*, #135 for annotation.

58.
Kadushin, A. Games people play in supervision. Social Work, 13(3): 23-32, 1968.

This article attempts to make explicit the variety of games most frequently played in supervision, reviewing the rationale behind gamesmanship, the ploys used, and the counter-games that have been devised. Games concerned with manipulating demand levels, redefining the relationship, reducing power disparity, and controlling the situation are detailed. Although the emphasis is on games developed by supervisees, the gamesmanship potential of supervisors is also suggested. Some techniques for dealing with games are also discussed.

Kolevzon, M. Notes for practice: Evaluating the supervisory relationship in field placements. Social Work, 24(3): 241-244, 1979. See *Research Studies in Field Instruction,* #137 for annotation.

59.
Manis, F. Openness in Social Work Field Instruction: Stance and Form Guidelines. Goleta, CA: Kimberly Press, 1979. See *Teaching/Learning Methodology,* p. 21, for cross-reference.

A research-based, six-stage model for developing and carrying out teaching-learning contracts between field instructors and students is provided. A set of guidelines are suggested to facilitate: openness in field instructor-student relationships; professional growth for the field instructor; mutuality between instructor and student; and the orientation and training of field students and instructors.

Marshall, C. "Social Work Students' Perceptions of Their Practicum Experience: A Study of Learning By Doing." Doctor of Education Thesis, Department of Adult Education, University of Toronto, 1982. See *Research Studies in Field Instruction,* #139 for Annotation.

60.
Matorin, S. Dimensions of student supervision: A point of view. Social Casework, 60(3): 150-156, 1979. See *Definitions of Field Instruction,* p. 3, for cross-reference.

Social workers new to supervision should evaluate how best to produce competent professionals who can master the complexities of current practice. A study examines the role shift the social worker must make from practitioner to field instructor in the context of new practice demands. Discomfort with authority and transference and coping with the students' dependency needs may strain the novice supervisor-student relationship. Flexible supervisors are receptive to broadening their repertoire and can take risks to revamp their skills. They serve as models for students to do the same. Several practice examples from mental health settings illustrate how to expose students to broader professional issues in their training.

Mishne, J. Narcissistic vulnerability of the younger student: The need for non-confrontive empathic supervision. The Clinical Supervisor, 1(2): 3-12, 1983. See *Particular Student Issues* #107 for annotation.

Munson, C.E. Style and structure in supervision. Journal of Education for Social Work, 17(1): 65-72, 1981. See *Research Studies in Field Instruction, p.* #141 for annotation.

Nelsen, J.C. Relationship communication in early field work conferences. Social Casework, 55(4): 237-43, 1974. See *Research Studies in Field Instruction,* #143 for annotation.

Nelsen, J.C. **Teaching content of early field work conferences.** Social Casework, 55(3): 147-153, 1974. See *Research Studies in Field Instruction,* #144 for annotation.

61.
Rosenblatt, A. & Mayer, J.E. Objectionable supervisory styles: Students' views. Social Work, 20(3): 184-189, 1975.

On the basis of autobiographical accounts collected from students, supervisory styles that students find offensive are depicted, and the ways they tried to cope with their dissatisfaction are described. Objectionable kinds of supervision were described as constrictive, amorphous, unsupportive, and therapeutic. The last named appeared the most stressful because it raised searching questions about the student's capacity to perform effectively. Because students were fearful of antagonizing their supervisors by openly voicing their grievances, direct confrontations were consistently avoided. Instead, students sought the help of their field advisor or engaged in "spurious compliance" with their supervisor. Suggestions are made concerning the amelioration of the strains.

Rotholz, T. & Werk, A. Student supervision: An educational process. The Clinical Supervisor, 2(1): 14-27, 1984. See *Research Studies in Field Instruction,* #146 for annotation.

Field–Class Integration
Field instructors and students frequently refer to the importance of the process of field-class integration, yet the literature focuses primarily on the student bringing material from the practicum to the classroom and integration taking place there under faculty auspices. The process of integration occurring in the practicum is rarely specifically discussed.

Olyan, S.D. Integration or divergence? Field instruction and the social work curriculum. The Social Worker: 57-61, Summer-Fall, 1979. See *Research Studies in Field Instruction,* #145 for annotation.

Rothman, J. Development of a profession: Field instruction correlates. Social Service Review, 51(2): 289-310, 1977. See *Context for Field Instruction,* #22 for annotation.

62.
Walden, T. & Brown, L.N. The integration seminar: A vehicle for joining theory and practice. Journal of Education for Social Work, 21(1): 13-19, 1985.

Integration seminars can be helpful in dealing with the dynamic tensions that develop between content in the classroom and in the field setting. A case is made for adopting this educational approach as a means for helping students derive practice principles, develop skills of critical self-analysis, demonstrate and benefit from peer learning, and arrive at a synthesis of theory and practice.

Teaching/Learning Methodology: Contracting & Evaluations
References are included with respect to the structure and process of field instruction. The majority of references focus on contracting and evaluations. Issues such as establishing learning objectives, and making a demand for work are discussed much less frequently and usually in the context of wider issues. The issue of field instructors and students terminating their relationship appears to have not been addressed in the literature.

63.
Armitage, A. & Clark, F.W. Design issues in the performance-based curriculum. Journal of Education for Social Work, 11(1): 22-29, 1975.

Performance-based curriculum designs are becoming more widely visible in social work education. This article describes the major features involved in design. Issues discussed concern the emphasis on skill objectives, the place of student and faculty individuation and creativity, the integration of learning experiences, and the assessment of performance.

64.
Brennen, E.C. "Evaluation of Field Teaching and Learning." In **Quality Field Instruction in Social Work,** pp. 76-97. Edited by B.W. Sheafor and L.E. Jenkins. New York: Longman, 1982.

Educational evaluation has the mutually supportive functions of teaching and grading. Both teacher and student resist evaluation in field education but it can be successfully accomplished through clearly-stated learning objectives and a structure which requires a series of examples of students work, together with rationale for their actions. Field instructors must be prepared to assess students' work and identify procedures to strengthen performance. The strengths and limitations of efforts to design rating instruments for field instruction are discussed.

65.
Clark, F.W. & Arkava, M.L. & Assoc. The Pursuit of Competence in Social Work. San Francisco: Jossey-Bass, 1979.

Practice effectiveness in diverse settings of social work will not be achieved rapidly or easily; it is an incremental process of change directed toward optimizing educational and professional objectives. This volume, based on a symposium, traces the origins of social work through to current models of practice; illustrates the range of viewpoints regarding critical variables defining social work competence; advocates teaching competencies that will allow practitioners to measure process and outcome; analyzes methodologies to make training in professional schools responsive to field practice; describes both the generalist approach and specialized competencies; and emphasizes that context plays a part in defining social work competencies.

Collins, D.G. "A Study of Transfer of Interviewing Skills from the Laboratory to the Field.: Ph.D. Thesis, Faculty of Social Work, University of Toronto, 1984. See *Research Studies in Field Instruction,* #131 for annotation.

Collins, D. & Bogo, M. Competency-based field instruction: Bridging the gap between laboratory and field learning. The Clinical Supervisor, 4(3), 1986 (accepted for publication). See *Research Studies in Field Instruction,* #132 for annotation.

66.
Coulshed, V., Woods, R. & Wiseman, H. "Failing to Fail Students: Views of Fieldwork Supervisors." Faculty of Social Work, Wilfrid Laurier University, 1985. Unpublished Paper.

The views of 103 supervisors, used by one university's school of social work, were sought to explore their experiences of students who had failed the placement. Attempts were made to establish on what grounds this decision had been based and how the evidence for the evaluation had been gathered. A preliminary questionnaire was completed by 53 supervisors, most of whom attended a half-day workshop where further descriptive data was gathered. Initial information on what constitutes practice incompetence and how the outcome is currently decided was collected. Some recommendations are offered to safeguard the rights of students, clients and other consumers, and those involved in the education process.

67.

Fox, R. Contracting in supervision: A goal oriented process. The Clinical Supervisor, 1(1): 137-49, 1983.

A contract based upon goals offers a powerful tool for supervision. This paper offers an outline for contracting with an actual illustrative example, and then provides two possible models for measuring the achievement of contract goals. Special circumstances for contracting are explored and the advantages discussed. The goal oriented contract approach emerges not only as a means to improve supervision, but also as a vehicle to measure effectiveness.

68.

Franigan, B. Planned change and contract negotiation as an instructional model. Journal of Education for Social Work, 10(2): 34-39, 1974.

To facilitate integration of the concepts of a purposeful planned change process and contract negotiation as integral parts of social work practice, a teaching model was developed whereby students were asked to design and implement a change process for themselves through the use of contracts. Use of this teaching model gave clear indication of students' understanding and integration of the planned change process.

69.

Freeman, E. The importance of feedback in clinical supervision: Implications for direct practice. The Clinical Supervisor, 3(1): 5-26, 1985.

Feedback can facilitate or hinder change and is important to the supervisory process. In order for it to be used effectively the conditions under which it is effective or ineffective must be understood. This article includes a review of some conditions which influence the effectiveness of feedback according to particular theoretical perspectives. A structured plan for providing feedback to students is described. Implications for students' direct practice activities are discussed.

70.

Gitterman, A. & Gitterman, N.P. Social work student evaluation: Format and method. Journal of Education for Social Work, 15(3): 103-8, 1979.

Student evaluation is an important and stressful task for field instructors. In a study, field instructors identified role strain emerging from difficulty with defining evaluation criteria, analyzing student practice, writing the formal evaluation and helping the student accept the evaluation. From their responses, a model was developed for the content and process of student evaluations.

71.

Green, S.H. Educational assessments of student learning through practice in field instruction. Social Work Education Reporter, 20(3): 48-54, 1972.

This article includes a brief historical review of the place of field instruction in the social work curriculum along with a discussion of problems inherent in judging student performance. Selected studies are reviewed as to the nature of competence and the evaluation process. A recommendation is made for field instruction to be viewed as a learning process in itself, not as a test for classroom knowledge.

Hamilton, N. & Else, J. Designing Field Education: Philosophy, Structure and Process. Springfield, Ill: Charles C. Thomas, 1983. See *Texts on Field Instruction*, #117 for annotation.

Manis, F. Openness in Social Work Field Instruction: Stance and Form Guidelines. Goleta, CA: Kimberly Press, 1979. See *The Instructional Relationship*, #59 for annotation.

Morton, T.P. & Kurtz, P.D. Educational supervision: A learning theory approach. Social Casework, 61(4): 240-46, 1980. See *Learning Theories*, #45 for annotation.

72.
Pennell, J. "Integration Model for Field Instruction: Training Manual." School of Social Work, Memorial University of Newfoundland, 1980. Unpublished Manual.

An overview of social work field instruction. Included are modules discussing how adults learn, models of field instruction, and some of the value-laden decisions encountered by field instructors in the dual role of teacher and agency representatives. Also included are discussion of basic "how to's" which guide the field instructor through four stages of the student's placement: pre-placement, beginning, middle, and end.

73.
St. John, D. Goal directed supervision of social work students in field placement. Journal of Education for Social Work, 11(3): 89-94, 1975.

A goal-directed paradigm for supervision of social work students in a field placement within a Veterans Administration Drug Abuse Program is presented. Included is an analysis of five phases in placement: screening, minimum orientation, goal work sheet, body of placement, and evaluation and closure. The concept of a goal work sheet is fundamental. This methodology was utilized with social work students over a two-year period and found to be useful.

Tropman, E.J. Agency constraints affecting links between practice and education. Journal of Education for Social Work, 13(1): 8-14, 1977. See *Context for Field Instruction*, #25 for annotation.

Educational Strategies

Tools for teaching and evaluation are referred to here including: the structure for field instruction of individual or group conferences; the use of process and/or summary recording, role playing, observed interviews, joint interviews and audio-video technology. The latter topic is occurring increasingly frequently in both the field instruction and social work supervision literature. There appears to have been minimal attempt to compare the relative efficacy of each educational strategy with the exception of research by Mayadas & Duehn (1978).

74.
Abels, P. "Education Media and Their Selection." In **Teaching and Learning in Social Work Education,** pp. 59-72. Edited by M. Pohek. C.S.W.E., 1970.

Media are extensions of the teacher, tools which can be used as educative devices for transmitting information among people and exposing students to planned learning experiences. Media must bring student, content, and teacher together and permit the student to relate to material on a personal level. Role-playing, the use of audio-visual equipment, and small group learning are discussed.

75.
Abels, P. "Group Supervision of Students and Staff." In **Supervision, Consultation, and Staff Training in the Helping Professions,** pp. 175-198. Edited by F.W. Kaslow and Associates. San Francisco: Jossey-Bass, 1977.

The use of the group for supervision is explored. The structural dynamics and patterns of supervisory groups are described and patterns that emerge in the practice of group supervision identified. Four phases involved in the change process: involvement, commitment, inquiry, and doing, are discussed.

Arkava, M. & Brennen, E.C., eds., **Competency-Based Education for Social Work: Evaluation and Curriculum Issues.** New York: Council on Social Work Education, 1976. See *Learning Theories*, #30 for annotation.

Barth, R. & Gambrill, E. Learning to interview: The quality of training opportunities. The Clinical Supervisor, 2(1): 3-14, 1984. See *Research Studies in Field Instruction*, #129 for annotation.

76.
Cowan, B., Dastyk-Blackmore, R. & Wickham, E.R. Group supervision as a teaching/learning modality in social work. Social Worker – Travailleur Social, 40(4): 256-61, 1972.

Group supervision can be used with staff members and students. The following phases of development occur: 1) pre-affiliation; 2) power and control, 3) differentiation; and 4) separation. For a group to meet its assigned functions, a contract must be clearly established, and the supervisor must accept his roles as authority figure and teacher. One experiment in group supervision produced the following conclusions: group supervision does not save time for the supervisor or learner, individual problems should not be handled in the group, personality differences must be handled as they come up.

77.
Goodman, R.W. The live supervision model in clinical training. The Clinical
Supervisor, 3(2): 43-49, 1985.

A live supervision model is presented in which the supervisor functions as both a
trainer and consultant in the ongoing therapy process. A rationale for this procedure
is given outlining the advantages of live supervision over traditional methods. Most
notably, the immediacy of the process allows the supervisor to train, intervene, and
evaluate simultaneously, to the benefit of both the client and trainee. Another unique
feature of this model is that the supervisor can also be part of strategic interventions.
Examples of live supervision strategies demonstrate the application of this model in
individual therapy.

78.
Hamlin, E.R. II, & Timberlake, E.M. Peer group supervision for supervisors.
Social Casework, 63(2): 82-87, 1982.

The peer-group supervision model is a response to the increasing emphasis on the role
of the middle-management supervisor. It is an outcome of a carefully structured group
whose members come together to understand the complexities and dynamics of the
supervisory process. Group transactions are designed to enhance supervisors' skill
and knowledge base, increase their sensitivity to changing emotional and learning
needs of supervisors, and to facilitate sharing of experiences. The use of the model by
field work supervisors in a large hospital is described. Limitations and benefits of
peer-group supervision are discussed.

79.
Kohn, R. Differential use of the observed interview in student training. Social
Work Education Reporter, 19(3): 45-46, 1971.

The observed interview can be used in a variety of ways to contribute to learning.
These are: the interview in which both student and supervisor are joined in the
process; one in which the supervisor observes from behind the one-way screen but does
not participate; and one in which a peer group of students observes, and may or may
not participate. Each of these methods has advantages and disadvantages.

Larsen, J. Competency-based and task-centred practicum instruction. Journal
of Education for Social Work, 16(1): 87-94, 1980. See *Learning Theories*, #42 for
annotation.

80.
**Mayadas, N.S. & Duehn, W.D. The effects of training formats and interperson-
al discriminations in the education of clinical social work practice.** Journal of
Social Service Research, 1(2): 147-161, 1978.

The relative effectiveness of three training formats (process recording, videotape
feedback, and videotape feedback with modelling) was examined using twenty-four
first-year graduate social work students. Findings indicate that videotape feedback
with modelling is the most effective training device for teaching specific interpersonal
behaviours.

81.
Mayers, F. Differential use of group teaching in first-year field work. Social
Service Review, 44(1): 63-70, 1970.

Three models are presented, analyzing content and method for teaching social work
students in the field. Use of small groups is proposed in conjunction with selected use
of the individual supervisory conference on an as-needed basis. The "cognitive" model

is used for orientation and accommodation to new content; the "affective" model for students experiencing initial or termination anxiety or conflict over social work knowledge and values; and the "work-group" model for developing effective task performance.

82.
Meltzer, R. School and agency co-operation in using videotape in social work education. Journal of Education for Social Work, 13(1): 90-95, 1977.

Videotape is a tool uniquely suited to record objectively the complexity and subtlety of human behaviour, which is the core knowledge base of social work practice. A collaborative format between the school and agency for the production of videotape records is discussed. Specific examples for involving the learner, both affectively and cognitively, through videotaped records are presented. The use of videotape play-back in the treatment process is considered, with particular attention to its applicability in such areas as self-confrontation, reality testing, enhancing self-esteem, strengthening identity, and improving communication.

83.
Rhim, B.C. The use of videotapes in social work agencies. Social Casework, 57(10): 644-50, 1976.

Advances in electronic technology, of which audiovisual equipment is one, have made inroads into the human service fields. The emergence of new knowledge and practice modalities has made traditional ways of training, supervision, and practice ineffective; and audiovisual equipment is increasingly being used to improve on the traditional ways. The use of traditional recording limits the scope of teaching and learning and thwarts active learning and the development of professional autonomy. Videotape play-back helps minimize these problems. The introduction of the equipment in one social agency is described.

84.
Rickert, V.C. & Turner, J.E. Through the looking glass: Supervision in family therapy. Social Casework, 59(3): 131-137, 1978.

A model which provides direct observation and immediate supervision is presented. Interviews are observed and coached through a one-way mirror by telephoning and convening a brief conference outside the interview, or entering the interview. Brief planning sessions are held before and after each interview. This model is contrasted with more traditional methods of supervision. Supervisory issues are discussed including selection of trainees, screening of cases, framing of directives, intrusiveness, and dependency. Clinical sequences illustrate the model.

85.
Schlenoff, M.L. & Busa, S.H. Student and field instructor as group cotherapists: Equalizing an unequal relationship. Journal of Education for Social Work, 17(1): 29-35, 1981.

The relationship of cotherapists has been shown to be the most important factor influencing the therapeutic process. The student/apprentice model for learning makes cotherapy an integral part of the educational process. In the training situation, however, an unequal status is inherent in the cotherapy dyad. Techniques to establish an egalitarian relationship are discussed including techniques to establish a relationship of mutuality, and techniques to create opportunities for student participation.

86.
Schur, E. The use of the co-worker approach as a teaching model in graduate student field education. Journal of Education for Social Work, 15(1): 72-79, 1979.

A student co-worker approach was initiated as a treatment aid in meeting the needs of large multi-problem families and groups as well as those of beginning graduate students; its continued use has demonstrated merit both in student learning and in the instructor's awareness of the process. It has served as a form of observed interview that has overcome the limitations of the traditional tutorial conference method. This paper describes the use of the co-worker approach as it has been applied to a graduate field education unit.

87.
Star, B. Exploring the boundaries of videotape self-confrontation. Journal of Education for Social Work, 15(1): 87-94, 1979.

Videotape self-confrontation is a training technique widely used in the helping professions yet realistic guidelines for its use have not been established. The effectiveness of such a tool is examined. The elements of a successful skill development program using self-confrontation are described.

Star, B. The effects of videotape self-image controntation on helping perceptions. Journal of Education for Social Work, 13(2): 114-119, 1977. See *Research Studies in Field Instruction,* #147 for annotation.

88.
Urdang, E. On defense of process recording. Smith College Studies in Social Work, 50(1): 1-15, 1979.

Process recording is a valuable teaching tool. It lends itself to disussion of interview content and interviewing techniques. Unlike video, it teaches the art of recall as well as "active integration" as the student emotionally and cognitively relives the interview, incorporating the observing ego of the supervisor. It also indicates what the student has grasped and what remains to be learned.

89.
Videka-Sherman, L. & Reid, W.J. The structured clinical record: A clinical education tool. The Clinical Supervisor, 3(1): 45-62, 1985.

The Structured Clinical Record, a clinical recording tool designed for social work students in field practice, is described and illustrated. This recording guide provides for systematic monitoring of case outcomes but goes beyond similar recording tools in two respects: it incorporates use of process data in the intervention process, and it is adaptable to the many theoretical frameworks and settings of social work practice. Application of the Structured Clinical Record is discussed.

Teaching/Learning Multiple Levels of Intervention

Literature regarding the practice component of field instruction refers almost exclusively to casework or micro practice. In this section, recognizing that some specific instructional issues arise, an attempt is made to include material relating to other levels of social work intervention, particularly community practice, administration, planning and policy making and research. References to field instruction in various fields of service and specific practice methodologies are not included here.

90.

Barbaro, F. The field instruction component in the administration concentration: Some problems and suggested remedies. Journal of Education for Social Work, 15(1): 5-11, 1979.

The need to prepare social work administrators for the field is now recognized. Problems pertaining to the development of field placements in administration are identified. A departure from traditional field models and school-agency relationships is suggested, including: a certificate program for field instructors; simulation games; an elitist model of leadership training; use of management consultants; faculty-led seminars for agency administrators; placement in the private sector; agency-based student units; and block placements.

91.

Barth, R. Professional self-change projects: Bridging the clinical-research and classroom-agency gaps. Journal of Education for Social Work, 20(3): 13-19, 1984.

Teaching students to use single-case research techniques is a worthy but difficult enterprise requiring much flexibility. This article describes several strategies to use in teaching such techniques and presents in greater detail the agency-based self-change project. In this approach, students work with supervisors in identifying, changing, and recording cognitions and behaviours salient to social work practice. The contributions of these projects to practice-research instruction are discussed.

92.

Campfens, H. "The State of the Art on Field Instruction and Skills Training for Community Development and Social Planning Practice: A Working Paper." Wilfrid Laurier University, 1981. Unpublished Paper.

A retrospective and futuristic view of community development and social planning field instruction and practice. Some issues and trends in the education for application of practice skills in community practice are discussed. Also discussed are principles in planning the field experience and the respective roles of student, field instructor and faculty. Concepts are operationalized with suggestions for: planning student field learning; performance evaluation; teaching and learning aids; and categories for community development and social planning placements.

93.

Epstein, L. Teaching research-based practice: Rationale and method. Journal of Education for Social Work, 17(2): 51-55, 1981.

Increasingly, courses are offered in social treatment that combine research, practice and field work. These courses appear to be a response to pressures to broaden the conceptual base in treatment and utilize research procedures. The problems of planning such courses are related to student disinterest, fears about loss of traditional skills, and uncertainty about the knowledge base. Three structures for making the combinations are suggested; each combination differs along a continuum of close to loose co-ordination of the various parts. Type I combines research, practice, and field work into one course; Type II is a semi-combined option with research and practice courses separate but co-ordinated, incorporating the field as a lab for research and practice, and; Type III co-ordinates separate research and practice courses, keeping field work separate.

94.
Grossman, B. Teaching research in the field practicum. Social Work, 25(1): 36-39, 1980.

Social workers tend to perceive a separation between research and practice and to attribute the separation to differences not just of methods, but of purpose as well, seeing the two activities as unrelated. If social work educators can relate research to the field experience, the potential value of research should become more apparent to social work students. This article reviews the Rothman model of social work research and development that suggests some innovations that would be useful for field teaching. Such experimentation requires an investment in resources. The potential rewards go beyond improving the image of research among students to enriching the relationship between practice and research-oriented faculty, enhancing the contributions faculty can make to agencies, and helping draw doctoral, master's, and undergraduate students together in shared projects.

95.
Lammert, M.H. & Hagen, J.E. "A Model for Community-Oriented Field Experience." In **Dynamics of Field Instruction,** pp. 60-67. New York: Council on Social Work Education, 1975.

A model is proposed for providing field experience to students interested in community-oriented social work directly under the auspices of a graduate school of social work.

Moore, D.E. "Helpline: An Integrated Field-Research Learning Experience." In **Dynamics of Field Instruction,** pp. 76-85. New York: Council on Social Work Education, 1975. See *Research Studies in Field Instruction, #140* for annotation.

96.
Neugeboren, B. Developing specialized programs in social work administration in the Master's degree program: Field practice component. Journal of Education for Social Work, 7(3): 35-47, 1971.

The experiences of a graduate school in developing a specialized program in social work administration with focus on the field practice components are described. Various issues are raised as to the feasibility of conducting such a program within the context of a graduate school of social work. Opportunities and constraints associated with agency-based field instruction and the variations in leadership potential of students are discussed.

97.
Rabin, C. Matching the research seminar to meet practice needs: A method for integrating research and practice. Journal of Education for Social Work, 21(1): 5-19, 1985. See *Research Studies in Field Instruction,* p. 43 for cross-reference.

A research seminar is presented as a model for matching research teaching to practice needs and maximizing the relevance of research for the practitioner. Assuming the behavioural principle of "successive approximation," skills are taught in a step-wise fashion that allows for gradually building competence in evaluating therapy research. In addition, experiential methods are used to allow for practice and cognitive/emotional changes to occur. It is proposed that changes in attitudes toward research are important and valid goals of the research seminar.

98.
Siegel, D.H. Can research and practice be integrated in social work education? Journal of Education for Social Work, 19(3): 12-19, 1983.

Preparing social workers to engage in empirically based social work practice has become a major trend in social work education. This article reports some of the findings from a study of the integration of research and practice in a graduate social work curriculum. Although students' scores on knowledge of research and statistics increased during their first graduate year, their scores on attitudes toward research became less positive. The author discusses possible explanations for this.

99.
Singer, C.B. & Wells, L.M. The impact of student units on services and structural change in Homes for the Aged. Canadian Journal of Social Work Education, 7(3): 11-27, 1981.

This paper describes and analyzes a model of education for direct practice in which skills for impact on the social services system are developed as an integrated part of practice teaching. As students assessed their clients' needs, the focus of problem identification moved back and forth between problems in the client system and problems in the organizational system; students were thus encouraged to express their professional commitment by implementing strategies for organizational change. This article discusses examples in which the field instructor and students had an impact on the service delivery systems; it analyzes the process of initiating and implementing such changes and evaluates the change.

100.
Vayda, E.J. Educating for radical practice. Canadian Journal of Education for Social Work, 102-106, Spring 1980.

The educator interested in radical practice is faced with the problem of when and how to give students a direct practice experience that will combine experiential knowledge of how major social institutions affect the lives of the poor with an organizing conceptual perspective. Social work students need to understand that behaviour and attitudes are shaped by social experience that is in itself a legitimate target for intervention yet the focus in the practicum tends to be the development of skills in assessment and intervention toward treating individuals and families. In order to expose students to clients who feel the restrictive coercive nature of the social system a preplacement practical experience was arranged at York University whereby beginning students were linked with a community legal aid program.

101.
Weeks, W. "Innovative Community Settings." First Occasional Paper, McMaster University, 1981.

Social work field education has expanded into innovative community settings which have emerged in response to newly visible groups and/or social issues, and to fill gaps in the provision of established social services. Field placements here offer an alternative form of social work education which involves some common processes, problems and possibilities for learning. Data was obtained from students, field instructors, and workers in innovative community settings in Canada and Australia. Areas discussed include: some theoretical dimensions of social work education in innovative community settings; examples of such settings and common organizational features; some of the contributions to and potential difficulties for social work student learning in such settings; suggestions for maximizing student learning; and other areas of mutual exchange and support between school and community.

Particular Student Issues

References here address student issues which present a specific challenge to field instructors. Included are references to students from minority cultural backgrounds; sexism and the field experience; the young narcissistic student; and the student and therapy. Additional specific situations such as field instruction and the exceptional/marginal/failing student, the young/mature student, and the disabled student occur only incidentally in the field instruction literature.

Behling, J., Curtis, C. & Foster, S.A. Impact of sex role combinations on student performance in field instruction. Journal of Education for Social Work, 18(2): 93-97, 1982. See *Research Studies in Field Instruction,* #130 for annotation.

102.
Benavides III, E., Lynch, M.M. & Velasquez, J.S. Toward a culturally relevant field work model: The community learning centre project. Journal of Education for Social Work, 16(2): 55-62, 1980.

The community learning centre was designed to develop culturally relevant student competencies for minority and non-minority field students and to identify the experiences that contribute to the development of such competencies. A questionnaire was developed and used to ascertain whether and how field instruction had contributed to the acquisition of culturally relevant student competencies in three categories: interpersonal, external-interactional, and culturally specific. Black, Hispanic, and Native American centres were involved in this project. Direct work with minority clientele and field seminars to facilitate the integration of multicultural content are recommended.

103.
Berkun, C. Women and the field experience: Toward a model of nonsexist field-based learning conditions. Journal of Education for Social Work, 20(3): 5-12, 1984.

The development of nonsexist field conditions is important because of the centrality of field experience to social work education. Using a systems approach, barriers to the natural evolution of nonsexist field conditions are identifed and characterized as institutionalized/structural, internal/personal and interpersonal/interactional. Because of the nature of the systems involved and the unlikelihood of evolutionary change, it is suggested that changes should be initiated by social work faculty. One recommendation is for content on women's issues and sexism to be part of the ongoing training of field instructors.

104.
Griffiths, K.A. Support systems for educationally disadvantaged students and assuring practitioner competence. Journal of Education for Social Work, 13(2): 38-43, 1977.

This paper addresses itself to an assessment of a number of student support systems developed and utilized in a three-year training effort with more than 104 Native American social work students at the University of Utah. Supports developed include related library materials; inclusion of minority content in the curriculum; activities to enhance self-image; socializing activities; special opportunities for small group interaction; opportunities for faculty to become involved; and ongoing structured evaluation of the program.

105.
Kahn, E.M. The parallel process in social work treatment and supervision. Social Casework, 60(9): 520-528, 1979.

Supervisors should understand the workings of the parallel process, a treatment impasse that occurs when similar emotional difficulties emerge simultaneously in supervisory and treatment relationships. Cognitive understanding and experiential modelling can be useful supervisory tools in helping to resolve the parallel process.

106.
Mayer, J.E. & Rosenblatt, A. Sources of stress among student practitioners. Journal of Education for Social Work, 10(3): 56-66, 1974.

Student practitioners experience considerable anxiety in dealing with their clients. This article, based on students' autobiographical accounts, seeks to locate the sources of their anxiety within a sociological frame of reference. Three inter-related sources of anxiety are considered: 1) the prescription to develop an "amicable" relationship with clients; 2) the desire to attain treatment objectives in the absence of adequate resources; and 3) the particular perspective that students bring to bear on their activities.

107.
Mishne, J. Narcissistic vulnerability of the younger student: The need for non-confrontive empathic supervision. The Clinical Supervisor, 1(2): 3-12, 1983. See *The Instructional Relationship*, p. 18, for cross-reference.

Schools of social work are increasingly admitting the younger student. The special needs of the younger, frequently narcissistically vulnerable student are most often demonstrated in the field practicum. Newer conceptions in narcissistic theory are offered to form an alliance between student and supervisor. Mishne postulates an increasing need for provision of "empathic" non-confrontive supervision.

Munson, C. Stress among graduate social work students: An empirical study. Journal of Education for Social Work, 20(3): 20-29, 1984. See *Research Studies in Field Instruction,* #142 for annotation.

108.
Ryan, A.S. Training Chinese-American social workers. Social Casework, 62(2): 95-105, 1981.

The learning needs of Chinese-American social workers are closely related to their cultural background. Four bilingual and bicultural issues—motivation for entering the social work profession, use of and response to authority, ethnic identity and self-esteem, and linguistic issues—and their implications for education are discussed.

109.
Santa Cruz, L.A., Hepler, S.E. & Hepler, M. Educationally disadvantaged students and social work education. Social Work, 24(4): 297-303, 1979.

Schools of social work are committed to the education of minority groups. However, many such students are educationally disadvantaged in the sense that their undergraduate training has not prepared them to deal with the educational procedures that are used in the profession's graduate schools. Means are suggested for resolution of this dilemma including "starting where the student is", tailoring each student's curriculum to his or her particular knowledge and capabilities, and adopting innovative approaches to teaching.

110.
Siporin, M. Teaching family and marriage therapy. Social Casework, 62(1): 20-29, 1981.

A major issue in teaching of family and marriage therapy in graduate schools of social work is how to help students attain technical competence and self development. Social work clinical courses have always had a mix of educational, supportive and personality development objectives. Traditionally, social work education has avoided direct therapeutic aid by instructors to students but of late confusion has arisen between education and therapy. Educators need to question overemphasis on therapy as an avenue to personal growth.

111.
Weinberg, L.K. Unique learning needs of physically handicapped social work students. Journal of Education for Social Work, 14(1): 110-117, 1978.

Recognition of physically handicapped social work students' unique learning needs and utilization of their experiences enhances classroom learning. Simulations can be structured to help them assess whether their handicap enters into the client-worker relationship and practice ways of dealing with possible client system responses.

Classic Articles and Texts: Pre-1970

These references are selected because of their particular relevance to field instructor training although they were published at a time when the need for such training, with few exceptions (Towle, 1954; Berengarten, 1961), was rarely clearly identified.

112.

Berengarten, S. Educational issues in field instruction in social work. Social Service Review, 35(3): 246-257, 1961.

The synthesis of total learning and metamorphosis from lay to professional person takes place primarily in field work. The role of the field instructor may be more challenging than that of social work supervisor as the latter deals with beginning workers who are self-reliant. To make the transition from practitioner to field instructor involves a different use of knowledge and reorientation to concept and theory. Schools must help practitioners become educators by acquainting them with the curriculum and developing their knowledge of educational theory and skill in teaching methodology. Seminars and workshops for beginning and experienced field instructors are recommended.

113.

Finestone, S. Selected features of professional field instruction. Journal of Education for Social Work, 3(2): 14-26, 1967.

Four selected criteria for field instruction are discussed: 1) a method of teaching that stresses conceptual learning using the field supervisor as model and student as apprentice; 2) a range of content that reflects the total social work curriculum; 3) preparation of the student for changes in knowledge base, organization of services, and methods of practice; 4) feedback of knowledge from field to class. To meet these criteria, a working partnership of class and field faculty is necessary.

114.

Hamilton, G. Self-awareness in professional education. Social Casework, 35(9): 371-379, 1954.

Self-awareness is important to professional development; the chief essential for its development is the student's capacity for self-acceptance. The field instructor must approach the problem of stimulating self-awareness through the practice experience. In Year 1 this involves helping the student shift his/her self-image from helper to social worker with emphasis on self-evaluation. The student begins to identify where his/her problems block him/her in learning how to help effectively; this requires the student to feel comfortable in the instructional relationship. In Year 2 the student learns to accept that he/she may have emotional problems which get in his/her way. The field instruction focus is to bring the student back to the experience of learning how to work with his/her feelings of inadequacy.

115.

Levy, C. A conceptual framework for field instruction in social work education. Child Welfare, 44(8): 447-452, 1965.

A framework is proposed clarifying the different responsibilities between graduate professional education and apprenticeship and between field instruction and agency supervision. The joint and several responsibilities of school, student, and field instructor are delineated.

116.
Towle, C. The Learner in Education for the Professions: As Seen in Education for Social Work. Chicago: University of Chicago Press, 1954.

A classic presentation on social work education from a psychoanalytic perspective. The objectives of professional training are clarified and the process through which the objectives are realized examined. The focus is on the student as the centre of the educational experience with "relationship" viewed as a means to facilitate learning. The teaching function is analyzed including preparation for the instructor and orientation and support for new instructors.

Texts on Field Instruction and Social Work Supervision

With few exceptions (Wilson, 1981; Sheafor & Jenkins, 1982; Hamilton & Else, 1983) there is a marked absence of general texts focusing specifically on field instruction. Additional texts annotated here refer to field instruction or student supervision in the course of discussing social work supervision.

117.
Hamilton, N. & Else, J. Designing Field Education: Philosophy, Structure & Process. Springfield, Ill: Charles C. Thomas, 1983. See *Teaching/Learning Methodology*, p. 21, for cross-reference.

Designed to help students, field instructors and faculty in social work and other human service education programs understand the structure of field education. Current concerns in field education are discussed. Field education is defined. The design of field education, its goals and objectives, structural issues, options in designing field education, and the placement and field co-ordination process are examined. Learning contracts, their rationale and their design are discussed in detail; a specific format is outlined including examples of exercises and feedback.

118.
Kadushin, A. Supervision in Social Work. New York: Columbia University Press, 1976.

An over-view of the state of the art of social work supervision. This book elaborates on the place of supervision in the social agency, the functions it performs, the process of supervision, and the problems with which it is currently concerned. The goal is to provide the knowledge base which is a necessary prerequisite to learning how to do supervision.

119.
Kaslow, F.W. and Associates. Supervision, Consultation, and Staff Training in the Helping Professions. San Francisco: Jossey-Bass, 1977.

A comprehensive guide to supervision, consultation, and staff training drawing from the fields of social work, psychiatry, psychology, sociology, and marriage and family therapy. Different approaches are discussed as well as specific supervisory techniques providing a reference for practical and theoretical issues.

120.
Munson, C.E., ed., Social Work Supervision: Classic Statements and Critical Issues. New York: Macmillan, 1979.

A comprehensive review of historical and current approaches to social work supervision drawn from a selection of technique-oriented as well as theoretical articles from 1903 to the present. Topics range from the first documented origins of supervision to the field's future trends, with special emphasis on organizational authority and professional autonomy.

121.

Munson, C. An Introduction to Clinical Social Work Supervision. New York: Haworth Press, 1983.

A detailed and comprehensive book about clinical social work supervision, for and about supervisors. Topics addressed include: a definition of supervision and its function; the history of supervision; supervisor styles and practitioners' reactions to them; technique in supervision; authority, structure and supervision; the evaluation of practice; burnout; audiovisual and action techniques; and supervision in different settings. An attempt is made to blend empirical research findings with case examples and comments made by supervisors and supervisees to form suggestions and recommendations for supervisors.

122.

Pettes, D.E. Staff and Student Supervision: A Task-Centred Approach. London: George Allen & Unwin, 1979.

A comprehensive book on supervision for staff or student supervisors. A detailed analysis is provided of the tasks undertaken and the problems faced by staff and student supervisors. A task-centred approach is presented to provide the supervisor with a firm base from which to maintain professional accountabiblity and responsible involvement. Ways of involving workers in a flexible two-way partnership with the supervisor are suggested. Supervision in casework, group work, community organization and residential work is compared. Developments in the preparation and teaching of prospective supervisors are discussed.

123.

Sheafor, B.W. and Jenkins, L.E., eds., Quality Field Instruction in Social Work. New York: Longman, 1982.

Provides a comprehensive view of the multiple dimensions of field instruction with the goal of assisting the integration of classroom and field instruction, co-ordinating the objectives from on-site field experience with those of the school's curriculum, and enhancing students' development as competent social work practitioners. Focused on are the following: the context of field instruction; field instruction as a curriculum unit; roles and responsibilities in field instruction; building blocks for good teaching; and the selection and development of learning tasks.

124.

Shulman, L. Skills of Supervision and Staff Management. Itasca, Ill: F.E. Peacock, 1982.

This book focuses on skills in communication, relationship, and teaching, and group leadership that supervisors and administrators in the helping professions need so they can direct the work of their staff more effectively. The author's objective is to provide clear, simple models of supervision practice to help new supervisors implement their complex human relationship tasks and help experienced supervisors understand why some staff contacts go well and others do not. Specific topics addressed include: the purpose of supervision and the supervisor's function; skills needed for the beginning and work phases of supervision; the educational function of the supervisor; group variations in supervision; the role of the supervisor between the staff group and external systems; feedback; evaluation and the ending phase.

125.

Waldfogel, D. "Supervision of Students and Practitioners." In **Handbook of Clinical Social Work,** pp. 319-344. Edited by A. Rosenblatt and D. Waldfogel. San Francisco: Jossey-Bass, 1983.

A review of supervision of students and practitioners with discussion of the overlap between the two processes as well as the distinctions. The major distinctive requirements of student supervision are: 1) the need for sharing the supervisory process with an outside institution and person; 2) the increased responsibility for containing anxiety; and 3) the central role of socializing the student into the profession. Also reviewed are: 1) the functions and history of supervision; 2) theories and principles of supervisory practice; 3) planning for supervision; 4) supervisory modalities; 5) supervisory tools; 6) formal evaluations; 7) the supervisory relationship; 8) social factors and roles; 9) ethics, and 10) consultation.

126.

Wilson, S.J. Field Instruction: Techniques for Supervision. New York: Macmillan, 1981.

A comprehensive, detailed over-view of field instruction. Content and style is highly pragmatic with major emphasis on the techniques of carrying out a field learning program. Focused on are the following: the structure of social work education and field instruction; selection of agencies and field instructors; needs and anxieties of students and field instructors; the process of field instruction; and process recording. Case examples are used throughout.

Research Studies in Field Instruction

Research studies annotated here range from those where there is limited data collection and analysis to those with much more extensive research design and attempts to control for the range of variables influencing the process of field teaching and learning.

127.
Amacher, K.A. Explorations into the dynamics of learning in field work. Smith College Studies in Social Work, 46(3): 163-217, 1976. See *The Instructional Relationship,* p. 17, for cross-reference.

Experiences of four first-year casework students in field work were studied in-depth. Each student attended a different school of social work and was placed in a different practice setting. Students and supervisors were interviewed frequently throughout the year. The research design used was a case-study technique. Categories that emerged for analysis included anxieties, context of learning, student-supervisor interaction, and situational factors. Some theoretical propositions were advanced that related anxieties, content, and the learning process. An examination of the relationship between learning and growth suggested they can be overlapping and complementary, but not synonymous. Some strains emanating from the marginality of social work as a profession, from problems in the knowledge base, and from the structure of one-to-one supervision were examined.

128.
Annett, A. & Pace, J. "A Consultative-Instructional Approach in Field Teaching." Faculty of Social Work, Wilfrid Laurier University, 1983. Unpublished Thesis. See *Approaches to Field Instruction*, p. 15, for cross-reference.

The purpose of this exploratory-descriptive study is to determine the extent to which social work students perceive that a consultative-instructional approach to supervision is a good learning experience in their field placement. In 1982, 50 social work students enrolled in the faculties of social work at Wilfrid Laurier and the Maritime School responded to a questionnaire measuring a number of teaching components. Findings indicate that the majority of students (58%) perceive that a consultative-instructional approach to field teaching is a good learning experience. A minority (42%) wanted the supervisor to do more than provide consultation.

129.
Barth, R. & Gambrill, E. Learning to interview: The quality of training opportunities. The Clinical Supervisor, 2(1): 3-14, 1984. See *Educational Strategies*, p. 23, for cross-reference.

This study examined social work students' opportunities to learn, practice, and sharpen interviewing skills. Master's students identified opportunities to observe interviewing models and to receive feedback on their own real or practice interviews. Students reported few opportunities to observe or listen to real, videotape, or audio tape models or to receive feedback on their interviews. Students judged interview training that included opportunities to observe effective models and receive feedback as most satisfying. These results indicate that the training of social work students may not include critical components of effective skill development. Reasons for this and possible correctives are discussed.

130.

Behling, J., Curtis, C. & Foster, S.A. **Impact of sex role combinations on student performance in field instruction.** Journal of Education for Social Work, 18(2): 93-97, 1982. See *Particular Student Issues*, p. 30, for cross-reference.

An empirical study was carried out between 1974 and 1978 at a large college in the midwest United States to test the impact of sex-role combinations on evaluation of students' field placement experiences. The findings imply that same sex-role combinations, in particular female student-female field instructor, are more positive generally than unlike combinations. The female student-male instructor was the most stressful and problematic; these stresses were attributed primarily to traditional sexist attitudes held by male instructors.

131.

Collins, D.G. "A Study of Transfer of Interviewing Skills from the Laboratory to the Field." Ph.D. Thesis, Faculty of Social Work, University of Toronto, 1984. See *Teaching/Learning Methodology*, p. 20, for cross-reference.

This study assesses whether students who learned basic interpersonal interviewing skills in a laboratory could transfer their learned skills to the field practicum. A number of areas related to the transfer question were also studied: the skill changes over the laboratory training period; demographic variables that may have contributed to learning and subsequent transfer; laboratory training compared to lecture training; and the methodological issue of equivalence of skill measures. Fifty-four students enrolled in a first-year laboratory course in an M.S.W. program were studied. The major finding is a lack of support for the transfer of learned interpersonal interviewing skills from the laboratory to the field practicum. Possible reasons for this are discussed.

132.

Collins, D. & Bogo, M. **Competency-based field instruction: Bridging the gap between laboratory and field learning.** The Clinical Supervisor, 4(3), 1986 (accepted for publication). See *Teaching/Learning Methodology*, p. 20, for cross-reference.

The effectiveness of laboratory training for teaching students basic interpersonal interviewing skills has been demonstrated. This article presents research on transfer of skill from the laboratory to the field; a comparison of laboratory and field learning; and recommendations for field instruction technologies to facilitate student transfer of skills from the laboratory to the field.

133.

Gelfand, B., Rohrich, S., Nevidon, P., & Starak, I. **An andragogical application to the training of social workers.** Journal of Education for Social Work, 11(3): 55-61, 1975. See *Learning Theories*, p. 12, for cross-reference.

Adults, according to Knowles, require learning situations adapted to their need to solve specific problems, an andragogical mode of learning based on self dependence. The results of a training course for workers in a children's aid society that was designed and implemented using andragogical principles are discussed. It was found, as predicted, that the workers improved their self-actualizing tendencies; they also increased their capacity to understand themselves and others. The workers preferred those training experiences that enlisted their involvement and participation over those of a less participative nature.

134.

Gitterman, A. "The Faculty Field Instructor in Social Work Education." In **The Dynamics of Field Instruction,** pp. 31-39. New York: Council on Social Work Education, 1975. See *Context for Field Instruction*, p. 7, for cross-reference.

This paper examines role strain as it is differentially associated with two statuses –agency and school-based field instructors. Data was collected from both groups of instructors. Findings include that faculty field instructors experience significantly greater role strain because of discrepant organizational expectations (service and training). Alternative models are suggested: the development of adjunct clinical professors simultaneously accountable to agency and faculty; and the direct administration of an agency by the school, allowing for effective co-ordination and integration of class and field.

135.
Kadushin, A. Supervisor-supervisee: A survey. Social Work, 19(3): 289-297, 1974. See *The Instructional Relationship*, p. 17, for cross-reference.

Despite the increasing importance of supervision as a unique responsibility of the professional social worker, relatively little research is available on social work supervision. This article is a report on a study of supervision conducted in 1973 of 750 supervisors, and 750 supervisees. The focus for the study were the sources of supervisory power, the satisfactions and dissatisfactions of supervision for both groups, and the functions of supervision. Some classical dilemmas of supervision were also examined including the way in which evaluation procedures are regarded and the legitimacy of the supervisors concern with the supervisees' personal problems.

136.
Kimberley, M.D. & Watt, S. Trends and issues in the field preparation of social work manpower: Part III: Educational policy, accreditation standards, and guidelines. Canadian Journal of Social Work Education, 8(1 & 2), 101-120, 1982. See *Context For Field Instruction*, p. 8, for cross-reference.

Emerging from Parts I & II of the C.A.S.S.W. series on Trends & Issues in the Field Preparation of Social Work Manpower were a variety of approaches to field instruction articulated by faculties. This resulted in a demand that C.A.S.S.W. make recommendations for educational policy, accreditation standards, and other guidelines regarding field preparation. Part III is a secondary analysis of the data regarding field instructors, field agencies, and field co-ordinators. Recommendations are made for educational policy regarding requirements for field preparation at the B.S.W. and M.S.W. levels. Recommendations are also made regarding accreditation standards with respect to: qualifications of field instructors in traditional and non-traditional placements; orientation of field instructors; time in the field; and selection of field placement agencies. Guidelines are discussed regarding field co-ordination roles; acknowledgement of field instructors and host agencies; and relations with agencies. Issues and recommendations that require further exploration are identified. Problems introducing policy, standards, and guidelines in an area where there is an academic/professional practice split are discussed.

137.
Kolevzon, M. Notes for practice: Evaluating the supervisory relationship in field placements. Social Work, 24(3): 241-244, 1979. See *The Instructional Relationship*, p. 18, for cross-reference.

Methodology, results and implications of research directed at understanding the nature of the supervisory relationship are presented. Forty-two students in a graduate school of social work were surveyed. The study found that students who were more critical of their supervisory relationship were more likely to engage in gamesmanship and that this was not effective in securing better evaluations. It was also found that faculty field instructors experience significantly greater role strain than agency-based instructors. Use of agency-based adjunct clinical professors and school-administered service systems are suggested structural alterations for more effective field instruction.

138.
**Larsen, J. & Hepworth, D. Enhancing the effectiveness of practicum instruc-
tion: An empirical study.** Journal of Education for Social Work, 18(2): 50-58, 1980.
See *Learning Theories*, p. 14, for cross-reference.

Practicum instructors play a strategic role in assisting students to gain the
competence essential to effective practice. A comparative study tested the efficacy of
traditional and experimental competency-based/task-centred methods of practicum
instruction. The study revealed that students taught under the latter method
performed at a higher level of competence and had more confidence in their skills than
those taught under the traditional method.

139.
Marshall, C. "Social Work Students' Perceptions of Their Practicum Experience: A
Study of Learning by Doing." Doctor of Education Thesis, Department of Adult
Education, University of Toronto, 1982. See *The Instructional Relationship*, p. 18, for
cross-reference.

The objectives of this descriptive, qualitative study are to identify the concerns of
students related to the practicum, the factors that helped and hindered learning, and
the nature of the learning derived from the practicum. The study is based on five
unstructured interviews with each of 22 first-year students enrolled in the same
faculty of social work. Data is analyzed in terms of common themes. Dominant themes
include: the scope of the assignment, the meaning of professional; relationships with
field instructors; and the integration of theory and practice. Relationship with field
instructor is the most dominant theme for all students. The most important finding is
the range in the quality of the experience as perceived by students. Recommended is:
the need for greater sensitivity to the needs of mature students; more attention to the
selection and training of field instructors; the importance of a supportive climate for
the risk taking inherent in experiential learning; the inclusion of a reflective seminar
in the curriculum; and the devotion of adequate resources to the practicum.

140.
Moore, D.E. "Helpline: An Integrated Field-Research Learning Experience." In
Dynamics of Field Instruction, pp. 76-95. New York: Council on Social Work
Education, 1975. See *Teaching/Learning Multiple Levels of Intervention*, p. 28 for
cross-reference.

A specific demonstration-research project that was undertaken as a requirement of
the field and the research curriculum at Dalhousie University Maritime School of
Social Work is described. The project's unique educational component was the
multi-dimensional nature of its learning experiences that related to all areas of the
school's curriculum.

141.
Munson, C.E. Style and structure in supervision. Journal of Education for Social
Work, 17(1): 65-72, 1981. See *The Instructional Relationship*, p. 18, for cross-reference.

A study of 65 supervisees and 64 supervisors addresses current issues in social work
supervision through exploring various models of structure, authority, and teaching.
Significant differences in level of interaction, supervision and job satisfaction, and
sense of accomplishment were found as the source of the supervisors' authority varied,
but no differences occurred in variations of structure. Incongruence between
supervisees' and supervisors' perceptions of actual and preferred structure, authority,
conference frequency and initiation, and context in supervision, demonstrates the
need for exploration of autonomy in practice and control in supervision.

142.
Munson, C. Stress among graduate social work students: An empirical study.
Journal of Education for Social Work, 20(3): 20-29, 1984. See *Particular Student Issues*, p. 31, for cross-reference.

A survey of 82 graduate social work students revealed low levels of physical and psychological stress associated with graduate work. Physical and psychological symptoms were reported at higher levels in relation to classroom work than in relation to field practice. No major differences in stress were reported on the basis of sex or marital status, but class standing did produce significant differences on the basis of practice performance variables. Analysis of the correlations between physical symptom variables and practice performance, agency climate, and supervision found that the highest proportion of correlations occurs among field instruction supervision. Implications of these findings for social work education programs are discussed. It is suggested that the relatively low levels of physical and psychological stress associated with field work can be attributed to the emphasis placed on supervision in field instruction.

143.
Nelsen, J.C. Relationship communication in early field work conferences.
Social Casework, 55(4): 237-43, 1974. See *The Instructional Relationship* p. 18, for cross-reference.

Supervisors' and students' relationship messages implying equality or authority were found to be patterned and associated with independently reported relationship strain. Relationship messages were noted in 68 conferences of 19 supervisor-student pairs. Most supervisors gave more peer-like messages in initial conferences, while students did so later. One-up, one-down, and mixed messages seemed to be negotiating devices. Pairs finally achieving relationship-message congruence at whatever level of authority or equality, and pairs in which students sent fewer peer-like messages tended not to report relationship strain. Seven pairs in which students sent more peer-like messages all reported strain.

144.
Nelsen, J.C. Teaching content of early field work conferences. Social Casework, 55(3): 147-153, 1974. See *The Instructional Relationship*, p. 19, for cross-reference.

Student and staff supervision are major vehicles for professional development yet the process has rarely been given research attention. Tapes of actual field work conferences were studied in relation to content of discussion, teaching techniques used and student responses to them. Findings suggested that these factors were mutually related and that placement setting, by influencing content, affected all three.

145.
Olyan, S.D. Integration or divergence? Field instruction and the social work curriculum. The Social Worker: 57-61, Summer-Fall, 1979. See *Field-Class Integration*, p. 19, for cross-reference.

Curriculum revision is a process engaged in by social work educators in an effort to keep their classroom offerings relevant to changing times and conditions. Within this process it appears that the field practice setting has remained relatively unaffected. Now that less faculty-based field instructors are available and the dependence of a social work school on the co-operation of agencies for field placement is increasing it is important that curriculum revision take more careful account of the capability of agencies to deliver the intended educational experience in the field practice situation. Two schools of social work are examined and a serious divergence between the expressed goals of the social work curriculum and the realities of the field practice situation was identified. A closer examination of the operating realities of school and agency with a view to adapting traditional modes of field practice is recommended.

Rabin, C. Matching the research seminar to meet practice needs: A method for integrating research and practice. Journal of Education for Social Work, 21(1): 5-19, 1985. See *Teaching/Learning Multiple Levels of Intervention*, #97 for annotation.

146.
Rotholz, T. & Werk, A. Student supervision: An educational process. The Clinical Supervisor, 2(1): 14-27, 1984. See *The Instructional Relationship*, p. 19, for cross-reference.

Supervision is an integral part of the educational process for student social workers. Educators and practitioners are becoming more aware of the need to develop improved methods to enhance this learning experience. This paper reports on a study of field instruction undertaken at McGill University in order to identify present methods and make recommendations for change. Particular attention was given to identifying the specific supervisory behaviours most and least valued by students and their supervisors.

147.
Star, B. The effects of videotape self-image confrontation on helping perceptions. Journal of Education for Social Work, 13(2): 114-119, 1977. See *Educational Strategies*, p. 26, for cross-reference.

Using videotape recordings to provide a self-encounter may yield valuable self-knowledge, difficult to obtain during ordinary student training, but important to professional development. A study was undertaken to determine the effectiveness of videotape self-image confrontation as a procedure to create changes in self-perceptions related to the helping process. Results indicated that a self-image confrontation produced significant amounts of perceptual change. While the initial impact was powerful, the effects of a single self-image confrontation tended to decrease over time. The findings suggested that effective use requires periodic and varied self-encounters throughout professional education.

148.
Thomlison, B. & Watt, S. Trends and issues in the field preparation of social work manpower. A summary report. Canadian Journal of Social Work Education, 6(2 & 3): 137-158, 1980. See *Context for Field Instruction*, p. 9, for cross-reference.

A study was undertaken to develop an initial understanding of the field practice component in the preparation of professional social workers in Canada based on research data from schools of social work and field settings across Canada. Objectives included: the identification and examination of issues facing schools of social work in the planning and implementation of field preparation programs; the facilitation of improved exchange, co-ordination and integration between education and practice in the field preparation process; and a common understanding of the role and place of field instruction in the preparation of social work manpower. Issues arising from findings include the costs and benefits of field instructor programs; the question of remuneration to agency; difficulties encountered by schools in the development and maintenance of field placements; communication between agency and school; alternate methods of field preparation such as lab and simulations; and, trends in field instruction.

149.
Watt, S. & Kimberley, M.D. Trends and Issues in the field preparation of social work manpower: Part II, Policies and recommendations. Canadian Journal of Social Work Education, 7(1): 99-108, 1981. See *Context for Field Instruction*, p. 10, for cross-reference.

Part I of the study, "Trends and Issues in the Field Preparation of Social Work Manpower," reported the results of a national study of field practice in Canada. The purpose of Part II is to discuss policy recommendations regarding the field preparation of social workers, arising from on-site consultations with faculty, field instructors and agency directors throughout Canada. Recommendations are made with respect to: field agencies; field instructors; selected dimensions of field placement; schools of social work and agency relations; operationalization of field preparation and costs and benefits of field preparation. An over-riding recommendation emerged from all consultations that C.A.S.S.W. must set standards in the field preparation of social work manpower. Areas for future research are identified.

Author Index

Campbell, M. "Consultation – The Essential Link in Social Work Field Program-mes." School of Social Work, Memorial University. Unpublished Paper. See #11.

Campfens, H. "The State of the Art on Field Instruction and Skills Training for Community Development and Social Planning Practice: A Working Paper." Wilfrid Laurier University, 1981. See #92.

Clancy, C. The use of the andragogical approach in the educational function of supervision in social work. The Clinical Supervisor, 3(1): 75-86, 1985. See #33.

Clark, F.W. & Arkava, M.L. & Assoc. The Pursuit of Competence in Social Work. San Francisco: Jossey-Bass, 1979. See #65.

Claxton, C.S. & Ralston, Y. Learning Styles: Their Impact on Teaching and Administration. Washington, D.C.: American Association for Higher Education, 1978. See #34.

Cohen, J. Selected constraints in the relationship between social work education and practice. Journal of Education for Social Work, 13(1): 3-7, 1977. See #12.

Collins, D.G. "A Study of Transfer of Interviewing Skills from the Laboratory to the Field." Ph.D. Thesis, Faculty of Social Work, University of Toronto, 1984. See #131.

Collins, D. & Bogo, M. Competency-based field instruction: Bridging the gap between laboratory and field learning. The Clinical Supervisor, 4(3), 1986 (accepted for publication). See #132.

Coulshed, V., Woods, R. & Wiseman, H. "Failing to Fail Students: Views of Fieldwork Supervisors." Faculty of Social Work, Wilfrid Laurier University, 1985. Unpublished Paper. See #66.

Cowan, B., Dastyk-Blackmore, R. & Wickham, E.R. Group supervision as a teaching/learning modality in social work. Social Worker – Travailleur Social, 40(4): 256-61, 1972. See #76.

Cowan, B. & Wickham, E. Field teaching in university context. Canadian Journal of Social Work Education, 8(3): 81-86, 1982. See #13.

Dastyk-Blackmore, R. Is field teaching supervision? Canadian Journal of Social Work Education, 8(3): 75-80, 1982. See #3.

Dea, K. "The Collaborative Process in Undergraduate Field Instruction." In **Under-graduate Field Instruction Programs: Current Issues and Predictions,** pp. 50-62. Edited by K. Wenzel. New York: C.S.W.E., 1972. See #14.

Dean, R.G. The role of empathy in supervision. Clinical Social Work Journal, 12(2): 129-139, 1984. See #55.

De Jong, C.R. "Field Instruction for Undergraduate Social Work Education in Rural Areas." In **The Dynamics of Field Instruction,** pp. 20-30. New York: C.S.W.E., 1975. See #26.

Dwyer, M. & Urbanowski, M. Field practice criteria: Valuable teaching/ learning tools in undergraduate social work education. Journal of Education for Social Work, 17(1): 5-11, 1981. See #35.

Eisikovits, Z. & Guttman, E. Toward a practice theory of learning through experience in social work supervision. The Clinical Supervisor, 1(1): 51-63, 1983. See #36.

Epstein, L. Teaching research-based practice: Rationale and method. Journal of Education for Social Work, 17(2): 51-55, 1981. See #93.

Fellin, P.A. "Responsibilities of the School." In **Quality Field Instruction in Social Work,** pp. 101-116. Edited by B.W. Sheafor and L.E. Jenkins. New York: Longman, 1982. See #15.

Finestone, S. Selected features of professional field instruction. Journal of Education for Social Work, 3(2): 14-26, 1967. See #113.

Fox, R. Contracting in supervision: A goal oriented process. The Clinical Supervisor, 1(1): 137-49, 1983. See #67.

Franigan, B. **Planned change and contract negotiation as an instructional model.** Journal of Education for Social Work, 10(2): 34-39, 1974. See #68.

Freeman, E. **The importance of feedback in clinical supervision: Implications for direct practice.** The Clinical Supervisor, 3(1): 5-26, 1985. See #69.

Frumkin, M. **Social work education and the professional commitment fallacy: A practical guide to field-school relations.** Journal of Education for Social Work, 16(2): 91-99, 1980. See #16.

Gelfand, B., Rohrich, S., Nevidon, P. & Starak, I. **An andragogical application to the training of social workers.** Journal of Education for Social Work, 11(3): 55-61, 1975. See #133.

George, A. "A History of Social Work Field Instruction." In **Quality Field Instruction in Social Work,** pp. 37-59. Edited by B.W. Sheafor and L.E. Jenkins. New York: Longman, 1982. See #1.

Gitterman, A. "The Faculty Field Instructor in Social Work Education." In The Dynamics of Field Instruction, pp. 31-39. New York: C.S.W.E., 1975. See #134.

Gitterman, A. "Comparison of Educational Models and Their Influences on Supervision." In **Issues in Human Services,** pp. 18-38. Edited by F.W. Kaslow and Associates. San Francisco: Jossey-Bass, 1972. See #37.

Gitterman, A. & Miller, I. "Supervisors as Educators." In **Supervision, Consultation, and Staff Training in the Helping Professions,** pp. 100-114. Edited by F.W. Kaslow and Associates. San Francisco: Jossey-Bass, 1977. See #38.

Gitterman, A. & Gitterman, N.P. **Social work student evaluation: Format and method.** Journal of Education for Social Work, 15(3): 103-8, 1979. See #70.

Gizynski, M. **Self awareness of the supervisor in supervision.** Clinical Social Work Journal, 6(3): 202-210, 1978. See #56.

Goodman, R.W. **The live supervision model in clinical training.** The Clinical Supervisor, 3(2): 43-49, 1985. See #77.

Gordon, M.S. "Responsibilities of the School." In **Quality Field Instruction in Social Work,** pp. 116-135. Edited by B.W. Sheafor and L.E. Jenkins. New York: Longman, 1982. See #17.

Green, S.H. **Educational assessments of student learning through practice in field instruction.** Social Work Education Reporter, 20(3): 48-54, 1972. See #71.

Griffiths, K.A. **Support systems for educationally disadvantaged students and assuring practitioner competence.** Journal of Education for Social Work, 13(2): 38-43, 1977. See #104.

Grossman, B. **Teaching research in the field practicum.** Social Work, 25(1): 36-39, 1980. See #94.

Hamilton, G. **Self-awareness in professional education.** Social Casework, 35(9): 371-379, 1954. See #114.

Hamilton, N. & Else, J. **Designing Field Education: Philosophy, Structure & Process.** Springfield, Ill: Charles C. Thomas, 1983. See #117.

Hamlin, E.R. II & Timberlake, E.M. **Peer group supervision for supervisors.** Social Casework, 63(2): 82-87, 1982. See #78.

Hawkins, F.R. & J. Pennell. "Training for Field Instructor Competence: Utilization of an Integration Model." Memorial University of Newfoundland, 1983. Unpublished Paper. See #7.

Hawthorne, L. **Games supervisors play.** Social Work, 29(3): 179-183, 1975. See #57.

Henry, C. St. G. **An examination of field work models at Adelphi University School of Social Work.** Journal of Education for Social Work, 11(3): 62-68, 1975. See #18.

Hersh, A. **Teaching the theory and practice of student supervision: A short-term model based on principles of adult education.** The Clinical Supervisor, 2(1): 29-44, 1984. See #8.

Horejsi, C.R. & Deaton, R.L. The cracker-barrel classroom: Rural programming for continuing education. Journal of Education for Social Work, 13(3): 37-43, 1977. See #27.

Jenkins, L.E. & Sheafor, B.W. "An Overview of Social Work Field Instruction." In Quality Field Instruction in Social Work, pp. 3-20. Edited by B.W. Sheafor and L.E. Jenkins. New York: Longman, 1982. See #49.

Jones, E.F. Square peg, round hole: The dilemma of the undergraduate social work field coordinator. Journal of Education for Social Work, 20(3): 45-50, 1984. See #19.

Kadushin, A. Games people play in supervision. Social Work, 13(3): 23-32, 1968. See #58.

Kadushin, A. Supervisor-supervisee: A survey. Social Work, 19(3): 289-297, 1974. See #135.

Kadushin, A. Supervision in Social Work. New York: Columbia University Press, 1976. See #118.

Kahn, E.M. The parallel process in social work treatment and supervision. Social Casework, 60(9): 520-528, 1979. See #105.

Kaslow, F.W. and Associates. Supervision, Consultation, and Staff Training in the Helping Professions. San Francisco: Jossey-Bass, 1977. See #119.

Kettner, P.M. A conceptual framework for developing learning modules for field education. Journal of Education for Social Work, 15(1): 51-58, 1979. See #39.

Kimberley, M.D. & Watt, S. Trends and issues in the field preparation of social work manpower: Part III educational policy, accreditation standards, and guidelines. Canadian Journal of Social Work Education, 8(1 & 2): 101-120, 1982. See #136.

Knowles, M.S. Innovations in teaching styles and approaches based upon adult learning. Journal of Education for Social Work, 8(2): 32-39, 1972. See #40.

Kohn, R. Differential use of the observed interview in student training. Social Work Education Reporter, 19(3): 45-46, 1971. See #79.

Kolb, D.A. Experiential Learning: Experience as the Source of Learning and Development. Englewood Cliffs, New Jersey: Prentice Hall, Inc., 1984. See #41.

Kolevzon, M. Notes for practice: Evaluating the supervisory relationship in field placements. Social Work, 24(3): 241-244, 1979. See #137.

Krop, L.P. Developing and evaluating a training manual for social work field instructors using elements of the behaviouristic system of learning. Arlington, VA.: ERIC Document Reproduction Service, 1975. See #9.

Krop, L.P. Developing and implementing effective modes of communication between the school of social work and agency-based faculty. Arlington, VA.: ERIC Document Reproduction Service, 1975. See #20.

Krop, L.P. A strategy for obtaining a performance-oriented training program for social work field instructors. Arlington, VA.: ERIC Document Reproduction Service, 1975. See #10.

Kutzik, A.J. "History and Philosophy of Supervision and Consultation: The Social Work Field." In Supervision, Consultation and Staff Training in the Helping Professions, pp. 25-59. Edited by F.W. Kaslow and Associates. San Francisco: Jossey-Bass, 1977. See #2.

Lammert, M.H. & Hagen, J.E. "A Model for Community-oriented Field Experience." In The Dynamics of Field Instruction, pp. 60-67. New York: C.S.W.E., 1975. See #95.

Larsen, J. Competency-based and task-centred practicum instruction. Journal of Education for Social Work, 16(1): 87-94, 1980. See #42.

Larsen, J. & Hepworth, D. Enhancing the effectiveness of practicum instruction: An empirical study. Journal of Education for Social Work, 18(2): 50-58, 1980. See #138.

Levy, C. A conceptual framework for field instruction in social work education. Child Welfare, 44(8): 447-452, 1965. See #115.

Lowy, L. Social work supervision: From models toward theory. Journal of Education for Social Work, 19(2): 55-62, 1983. See #43.

Manis, F. Openness in Social Work Field Instruction: Stance and Form Guidelines. Goleta: CA: Kimberly Press, 1979. See #59.

Markowski, E.M. & Cain, H.I. Marital and family therapy training and supervision: A regional model for rural mental health. The Clinical Supervisor, 1(1): 65-75, 1983. See #28.

Marshall, C. "Social Work Students' Perceptions of Their Practicum Experience: A Study of Learning by Doing." Doctor of Education Thesis, Department of Adult Education, University of Toronto, 1982. See #139.

Matching Teaching & Learning Styles. Theory into Practice, Winter 1984. See #44.

Matorin, S. Dimensions of student supervision: A point of view. Social Casework, 60(3): 150-156, 1979. See #60.

Mayadas, N.S. & Duehn, W.D. The effects of training formats and interpersonal discriminations in the education of clinical social work practice. Journal of Social Service Research, 1(2): 147-161, 1978. See #80.

Mayer, J.E. & Rosenblatt, A. Sources of stress among student practitioners. Journal of Education for Social Work, 10(3): 56-66, 1974. See #106.

Mayers, F. Differential use of group teaching in first-year field work. Social Service Review, 44(1): 63-70, 1970. See #81.

Meltzer, R. School and agency co-operation in using videotape in social work education. Journal of Education for Social Work, 13(1): 90-95, 1977. See #82.

Mishne, J. Narcissistic vulnerability of the younger student: The need for non-confrontive empathic supervision. The Clinical Supervisor, 1(2): 3-12, 1983. See #107.

Moore, D.E. "Help Line: An Integrated Field-research Learning Experience." In The Dynamics of Field Instruction, pp. 76-85. New York: C.S.W.E., 1975. See #140.

Morton, T.D. & Kurtz, P.D. Educational supervision: A learning theory approach. Social Casework, 61(4): 240-246, 1980. See #45.

Munson, C.E., Ed. Social Work Supervision: Classic Statements and Critical Issues. New York: MacMillan, 1979. See #120.

Munson, C.E. Style and structure in supervision. Journal of Education for Social Work, 17(1): 65-72, 1981. See #141.

Munson, C. An Introduction to Clinical Social Work Supervision. New York: Haworth Press, 1983. See #121.

Munson, C. Stress among graduate social work students: An empirical study. Journal of Education for Social Work, 20(3): 20-29, 1984. See #142.

Murdaugh, J. Brief notes: Student supervision unbound. Social Work, 19(2): 131-132, 1974. See #4.

Nelsen, J.C. Relationship communication in early fieldwork conferences. Social Casework, 55(4): 237-43, 1974. See #143.

Nelsen, J.C. Teaching content of early fieldwork conferences. Social Casework, 55(3): 147-153, 1974. See #144.

Neugeboren, B. Developing specialized programs in social work administration in the Master's degree program: Field practice component. Journal of Education for Social Work, 7(3): 35-47, 1971. See #96.

Olyan, S.D. Integration or divergence? Field instruction and the social work curriculum. The Social Worker, 57-61, Summer-Fall, 1979. See #145.

Pennell, J. "Integration Model for Field Instruction: Training Manual." School of Social Work, Memorial University of Newfoundland, 1980. Unpublished Paper. See #72.

Pettes, D.E. Staff and Student Supervision: A Task-Centred Approach. London: George Allen & Unwin, 1979. See #122.

Price, H.G. Achieving a balance between self-directed and required learning. Journal of Education for Social Work, 12(1): 105-112, 1976. See #46.

Rabin, C. Matching the research seminar to meet practice needs: A method for integrating research and practice. Journal of Education for Social Work, 21(1): 5-19, 1985. See #97.

Rhim, B.C. The use of videotapes in social work agencies. Social Casework, 57(10): 644-50, 1976. See #83.

Rickert, V.C. & Turner, J.C. Through the looking glass: Supervision in family therapy. Social Casework, 59(3): 131-137, 1978. See #84.

Rosenblatt, A. & Mayer, J.E. Objectionable supervisory styles: Students' views. Social Work, 20(3): 184-189, 1975. See #61.

Rosenblum, A.F. & Raphael, F.B. The role and function of the faculty-field liaison. Journal of Education for Social Work, 19(1): 67-73, 1983. See #21.

Rothman, B. Perspectives on learning and teaching in continuing education. Journal of Education for Social Work, 9(2): 39-52, 1973. See #17.

Rothman, J. Development of a profession: Field instruction correlates. Social Service Review 51(2): 289-310, 1977. See #22.

Rotholz, T. & Werk, A. Student supervision: An educational process. The Clinical Supervisor, 2(1): 14-27, 1984. See #146.

Ryan, A.S. Training Chinese-American social workers. Social Casework, 62 (2): 95-105, 1981. See #108.

St. John, D. Goal directed supervision of social work students in field placement. Journal of Education for Social Work, 11(3): 89-94, 1975. See #73.

Santa Cruz, L.A., Hepler, S.E. & Hepler, M. Educationally disadvantaged students and social work education. Social Work, 24(4): 297-303, 1979. See #109.

Schlenoff, M.L. & Busa, S.H. Student and field instructor as group cotherapists: Equalizing an unequal relationship. Journal of Education for Social Work, 17(1): 29-35, 1981. See #85.

Schur, E. The use of the coworker approach as a teaching model in graduate student field education. Journal of Education for Social Work, 15(1): 72-79, 1979. See #86.

Schutz, M.L. & Gordon, W.E. Reallocation of educational responsibility among schools, agencies, students and NASW. Journal of Education for Social Work, 13(2): 99-106, 1977. See #23.

Sheafor, B.W. & L.E. Jenkins. Issues that affect the development of a field instruction curriculum. Journal of Education for Social Work, 17(1): 12-20, 1981. See #24.

Sheafor, B.W. & Jenkins, L.E. Quality Field Instruction in Social Work. New York: Longman, 1982. See #123.

Shulman, L. Skills of Supervision and Staff Management. Itasca, Ill: F.E. Peacock, 1982. See #124.

Siegel, D.H. Can research and practice be integrated in social work education? Journal of Education for Social Work, 19(3): 12-19, 1983. See #98.

Singer, C.B. & Wells, L.M. The impact of student units on services and structural change in Homes for the Aged. Canadian Journal of Social Work Education, 7(3): 11-27, 1981. See #99.

Siporin, M. Teaching family and marriage therapy. Social Casework, 62(1): 20-29, 1981. See #110.

Siporin, M. "The Process of Field Instruction." In **Quality Field Instruction in Social Work**, pp. 175-197. Edited by B.W. Sheafor and L.E Jenkins New York: Longmans, 1982. See #50.

Somers, M.L. **Contributions of learning and teaching theories to the explication of the role of the teacher in social work education.** Journal of Education for Social Work, 5(2): 61-73, 1979. See #48.

Somers, M.L. **Dimensions and Dynamics of Engaging the Learner.** Journal of Education for Social Work, 7(3): 49-57, 1971. See #51.

Star, B. **The effects of videotape self-image confrontation on helping perceptions.** Journal of Education for Social Work, 13(2): 114-119, 1977. See #147.

Star, B. **Exploring the boundaries of videotape self-confrontation.** Journal of Education for Social Work, 15(1): 87-94, 1979. See #87.

Thomlison, B. & Watt, S. **Trends and issues in the field preparation of social work manpower: A summary report.** Canadian Journal of Social Work Education, 6(2 & 3): 137-158, 1980. See #148.

Towle, C. **The Learner in Education for the Professions: As Seen in Education for Social Work.** Chicago: University of Chicago Press, 1954. See #116.

Tropman, E.J. **Agency constraints affecting links between practice and education.** Journal of Education for Social Work, 13(1): 8-14, 1977. See #25.

Urdang, E. **On defense of process recording.** Smith College Studies in Social Work, 50(1): 1-15, 1979. See #88.

Vayda, E.J. **Educating for radical practice.** Canadian Journal of Education for Social Work, 102-106, Spring 1980. See #100.

Videka-Sherman, L. & Reid, W.J. **The structured clinical record: A clinical education tool.** The Clinical Supervisor, 3(1): 45-62, 1985. See #89.

Walden, T. & Brown, L.N. **The integration seminar: A vehicle for joining theory and practice.** Journal of Education for Social Work, 21(1): 13-19, 1985. See #62.

Waldfogel, D. "Supervision of Students and Practitioners." In **Handbook of Clinical Social Work**, pp. 319-344. Edited by A. Rosenblatt and D. Waldfogel. San Francisco: Jossey-Bass, 1983. See #125.

Watt, S & Kimberley, M.D. **Trends and issues in the field preparation of social work manpower: Part II, policies and recommendations.** Canadian Journal of Social Work Education, 7(1): 99-108, 1981. See #149.

Webb, N.B. **Developing competent clinical practitioners: A model with guidelines for supervisors.** The Clinical Supervisor, 1(4): 41-53, 1983. See #52.

Weber, G.K. **Preparing social workers for practice in rural social systems.** Journal of Education for Social Work, 12(3): 108-115, 1976. See #29.

Weeks, W. "Innovative Community Settings." First Occasional Paper, McMaster University, 1981. See #101.

Weinberg, L.K. **Unique learning needs of physically handicapped social work students.** Journal of Education for Social Work, 14(1): 110-117, 1978. See #111.

Wijnberg, M.H. & Schwartz, M.C. **Models of student supervision: The apprentice, growth, and role systems models.** Journal of Education for Social Work, 13(3): 107-113, 1977. See #53.

Wilson, S.J. **Field Instruction: Techniques for Supervision.** New York: Macmillan, 1981. See #126.